Ingratitude

An account of Missionaries in the Earthquake on May 31, 1970, in Ancash Peru

LEO JAY SMITH

outskirts press

PREFACE

This book is an account of a devastating earthquake that occurred in Peru on Sunday, May 31, 1970. I included stories of some of the LDS missionaries that were most affected by the event in chapter eight. The material came from interviews by the mission leaders with those involved the week after the quake, which they compiled into a booklet, named Earthquake. I was fascinated by the story two years later, when I was a missionary in Peru. I have reorganized the material to the timeline of the nine days following the earthquake. It is just happenstance that I did it on the fiftieth anniversary of the disaster. The first seven chapters of this book give background information that may help the reader understand the story.

At least once a month, while I was in Peru, it was common to feel an earth tremor. The immediate question always was: Is this going to be a bad one? There have been twenty-three earthquakes of magnitude over 6.0 between 1970 and 2019 in Peru.

"The earthquake, however, must be to everyone a most impressive event: the earth, considered from our earliest childhood as the type of solidity, has oscillated like a thin crust beneath our feet; and in seeing the laboured works of man in a moment overthrown, we feel the insignificance of his boasted power."

— **Charles Darwin, <u>Voyage of the Beagle</u>**

Index

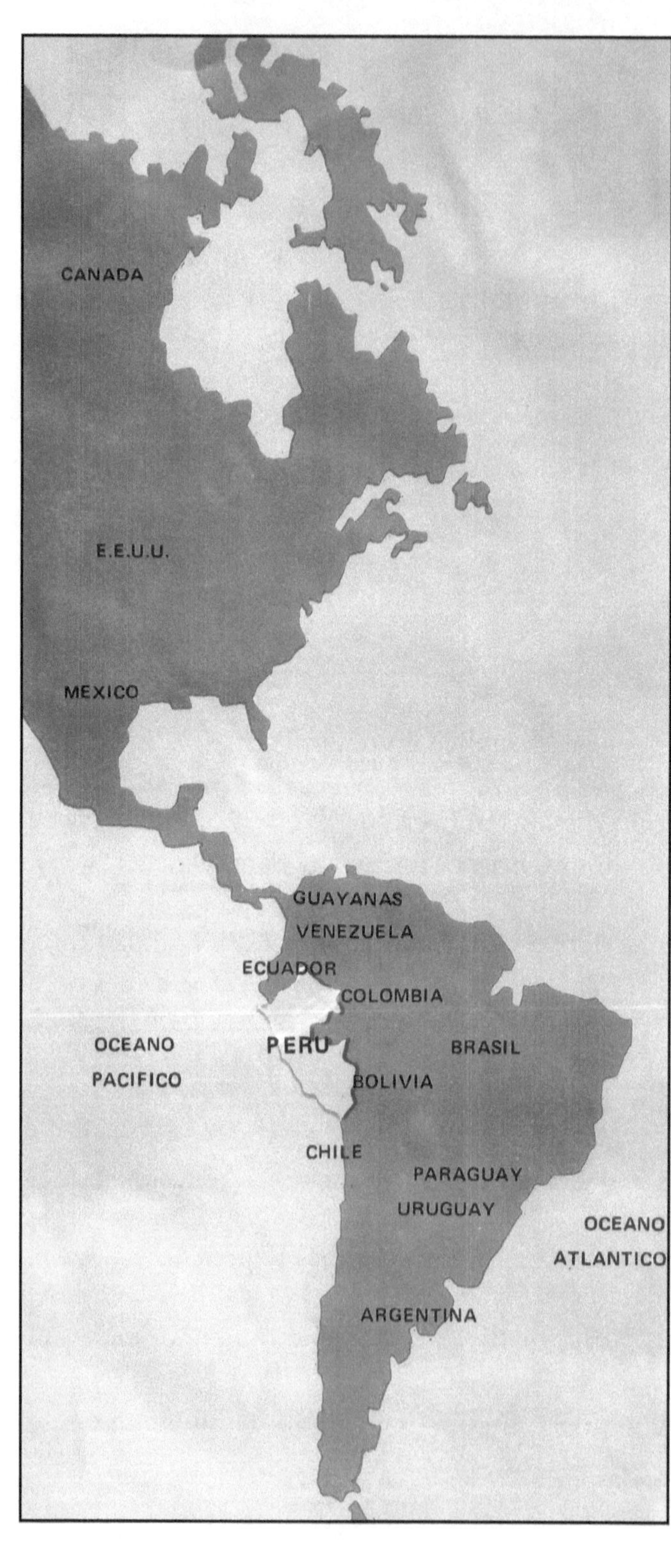

CANADA
E.E.U.U.
MEXICO
GUAYANAS
VENEZUELA
ECUADOR
COLOMBIA
OCEANO
PACIFICO
PERU
BRASIL
BOLIVIA
CHILE
PARAGUAY
URUGUAY
OCEANO
ATLANTICO
ARGENTINA

Chapter 1

LOCATIONS IN THIS STORY

Peru

SOUTH AMERICA IS the fourth largest continent in the world and covers an area of 6.9 million square miles. There are 12 sovereign countries: Colombia, Bolivia, Argentina, Chile, Peru, Uruguay, Brazil, Paraguay, Venezuela, Guyana, Suriname, and Ecuador. Peru is the third-largest country, with an area of just under 0.5 million square miles.

The Republic of Peru is on the western coast of South America. It is bordered in the north by Ecuador and Colombia, in the east by Brazil, in the southeast by Bolivia, in the south by Chile, and in the west by the Pacific Ocean. The country has very diverse eco-systems, with habitats ranging from the arid plains of the Pacific coastal region in the west to the tropical Amazon Basin rainforest in the east, including the Amazon river, to the peaks of the Andes mountains vertically extending from the north to the southeast of the country.

The history of Peru spans four millennia, extending back through several stages of cultural development in the mountain region and the lakes. The area was home to the Norte Chico civilization, which was the oldest civilization in the Americas and one of the six oldest in the world, and to the Inca Empire, the largest and most advanced state in Pre-Columbian America. The area was conquered by the Spanish Empire in the 16th century, which established a Viceroyalty in Lima with jurisdiction over most of its South American domains. The nation declared independence from Spain in 1821. The following 100 years included several territory disputes between Peru, Bolivia, and Chile.

Throughout Latin America in the 1960s, communist movements inspired by the Cuban Revolution sought to win power through guerrilla warfare. The Revolutionary Left Movement, or MIR, launched a rebellion that had been crushed by 1965, but Peru's internal strife would only accelerate until its climax in the 1990s.

The military has been prominent in Peruvian history. Coups have repeatedly interrupted civilian constitutional government. A recent period of military rule (1968–1980) began when General Juan Velasco Alvarado overthrew elected President Fernando Belaúnde Terry of the Popular Action Party (AP.) As part of what has been called the "first phase" of the military government's nationalist program, Velasco undertook an extensive agrarian reform program and nationalized the fish meal industry, some petroleum companies, and several banks and mining firms.

Peru consists of twenty-four administrative regions or departments, which are governed by Regional Governments. The provinces are subdivisions of the larger regions. The districts are third-level country subdivisions of the Provinces.

The following map shows the locations of the main cities in this account: Lima, Chimbote, Caraz, Yungay, and Huaraz:

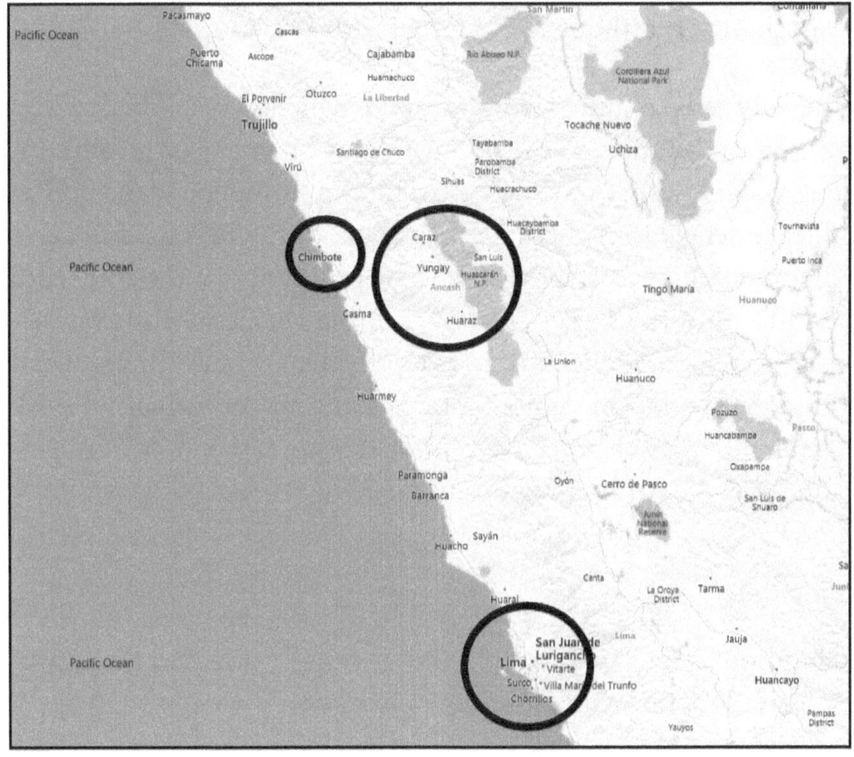

Lima

Lima is a Region that has Lima as a Province and is administered from the city of Lima.

The Ichma society established the city in the valley of the Rímac River. It was formed around 1100 AD following the breakup of the Wari Empire and lasted until around 1440 when the Inca Empire overthrew them.

After Francisco Pizarro defeated the Inca Empire, he founded Spanish Lima on January 18, 1535. The city became the capital of the Viceroyalty of Peru and the site of a Real Audiencia, which was an appellate court of Spain in 1543. In the 17th century, the city prospered as the center of an extensive trade network despite damage from earthquakes and the threat of pirates.

The city was required to provide payments for Royalist and Patriot armies alike, so the population of Lima played an ambivalent role in the 1821–1824 Peruvian War of Independence. After independence, Lima became the capital of the Republic of Peru. The town enjoyed a short period of prosperity in the mid-19th century until the 1879–1883 War of the Pacific when it was occupied and looted by Chilean troops. After the war, the city went through a period of demographic expansion and urban renewal. Population growth accelerated in the 1940s, spurred by immigration from the Andean regions of Peru.

Chimbote

Chimbote is the largest city in the Ancash Region and the capital of Santa Province and Chimbote District.

The city is on the coast in Ferrol Bay, 130 kilometers (80 miles) south of Trujillo, and 420 kilometers (260 miles) north of Lima on the North Pan-American highway. It is the start of a chain of important cities on the Peruvian north coast which are Trujillo, Chiclayo, and Piura.

The advantages of this geographic location made Chimbote into a transshipment junction for the Santa River valley. The Santa River begins from Lake Conococha and, for 200 kilometers (124 miles,) runs in a northerly direction between the Cordillera Negra in the west and the Cordillera Blanca in the east, forming the fertile Callejón de Huaylas. At 2,000 meters (6562 feet) above sea level, the river changes its course to a westerly direction, squeezing through the narrow gorge of Cañon del Pato ("Duck's Canyon") before it finally breaks through the coastal ridges.

The opening of the Pan-American Highway created easy access to Lima in the 1930s. In 1940 Chimbote was still a small fishing port, with only 2,400 inhabitants. In 1943, the government created the Corporación Peruana del Santa (Peruvian Corporation of Santa) which assumed ownership of the railroad, made improvements to the port, and began work on a hydroelectric power station on the Río Santa in the Cañón del Pato in Huallanca. In 1958, the first stage of the power station was completed. Also, in 1943 iron and steel plants were built. By then, the first companies dedicated to the extraction of fish oil from the Pacific bonito fish arrived in the area, which was sold for a high price abroad due to World War II. By 1970 there was a factory to convert anchovies into fish meal south of the city.

Between 1960 and 1970, Chimbote's population multiplied by more than a hundred times. By the early 1970's less than 5 percent of the people from Chimbote would genuinely consider themselves as a native of the city.

Caraz

Caraz is a town in the Caraz District in the southeastern part of Huaylas Province of the Ancash Region in Peru.

The town is in the Cordillera Blanca (Spanish for white range) mountain range and located at an elevation of about 2250 meters (7428 feet). It has the traditional architecture and lifestyle of an Andean village. The1970 Ancash earthquake destroyed the remaining cities in the valley.

Caraz is still a popular destination for trekking and day walks into the Huascaran National Park, and offers a much quieter and safer option when compared with Huaraz. The weather (due to the altitude) is gentle and provides a comfortable stay.

Yungay

Yungay is a town in the Yungay District in the Yungay Province of the Ancash Region in Peru.

It is 450 kilometers (500 miles) north of Lima and located in the Callejón de Huaylas on Río Santa. The elevation is approximately 2,500 meters (8200 feet.) East of the small town is the mountain ridges of the snow-covered Cordillera Blanca, with Huascarán, Peru's highest mountain, no more than 15 kilometers (9 miles) east of Yungay.

In 1962 two American scientists, David Bernays and Charles Sawyer, had reported seeing a massive vertical slab of rock being undermined by a glacier, which threatened to fall and cause the obliteration of Yungay. According to Sawyer, when their observation was reported in the *Espreso* newspaper (27 September 1962), the government ordered them to retract or face prison, and they fled the country. The government forcibly prevented citizens from speaking of an impending disaster. Eight years later, the prediction came true. On May 31, 1970, the Ancash earthquake caused a substantial part of the north side of a mountain, Nevado Huascarán, to collapse and dislodged an unstable mass of glacial ice.

The Peruvian government declared the buried city a national cemetery and has forbidden excavation in the area. The current town was rebuilt one mile north of the destroyed city.

Huascarán

Huascarán is a mountain in the Peruvian province of Yungay, situated in the Cordillera Blanca range of the western Andes. The highest southern summit of Huascarán (Huascarán Sur) is the highest point in Peru and is the fourth highest mountain in the Western Hemisphere and South America. The peak was named after Huáscar, a 16th-century Inca emperor who was the Sapa Inca (emperor) of the Inca empire.

Huaraz

Huaraz is a town in the Huaraz District in the Huaraz Province of the Ancash Region in Peru. Huaraz is located in the middle of the Huaylas Valley and on the right side of the Santa River.

The city has an elevation of approximately 3050 meters (10,007 feet) above sea level. It was founded before the Inca Empire when humans settled around the valley of the Santa River and Qillqay. Spanish occupation occurred in 1574, and they set up the town as a Spanish-indigenous reducción, which is a community under ecclesiastical or royal authority to facilitate colonization. Jesuit missionaries and other colonial administrators attempted to convert the natives to Christianity and to teach them better farming methods and simple crafts.

During the war for the independence of Peru, the whole city supported the Liberating Army with food and guns, earning the city the title of "Noble and Generous City" granted by Simón Bolívar.

The city is the seat of the province's Roman Catholic Bishop and the site of the cathedral. It is also the leading financial and trade center of the Callejón de Huaylas.

Huaraz is a tourist destination for winter sports and adventure. Many visitors from around the world come to the city to practice sports like climbing, hiking, mountain biking, and snowboarding, and also to visit the glaciers and mountains of the Cordillera Blanca, mainly Mount Huascarán. Along with the snowy peaks of the Cordillera Blanca, one can visit archaeological sites like Chavín de Huantar and the eastern mountains of Ancash, known as Conchucos.

In 1970, the earthquake destroyed 95% of the city along with much of the Ancash Region. The town received much foreign assistance from many countries. For this reason, it was named a "Capital of International Friendship."

Chapter 2

THE CATHOLIC CHURCH IN PERU

THE SPANISH CONQUISTADORS not only subjugated Peru militarily but also sought to convert the indigenous populations to Christianity. The Catholic church built some convents on Inca sites to suppress the Indigenous Andean religious beliefs and practices. For example, in 1605, Dominican nuns built the Convent of Santa Catalina in Cuzco atop the location of the "acllahuasi," once home to virginal young women dedicated to serving the ruling Inca. The Convent of Santa Clara was one of the first institutions the conquistadores of Cuzco built for "Indian nobles," the daughters of the indigenous elite whose collaboration made Spain's indirect rule over the Andes possible. At Santa Clara, Inca nobles were to be "raised" Christian and were to learn "buenas costumbres" (literally, good customs or manners), which was shorthand for education in "Spanishness." After graduating from this course, charges were free to profess vows or leave the convent. Many prominent Spanish men lived with elite Inca women, only to marry Spanish women and then later in life marry off their

Andean partners to less well-known Spaniards.

Today, the Peruvian government is closely allied with the Catholic Church. Article 50 of the Constitution recognizes the Catholic Church's role as "an important element in the historical, cultural, and moral development of the nation." Catholic clergy and laypersons receive state remuneration in addition to the stipends paid to them by the Church. The payment applies to the country's 52 bishops, as well as to some priests whose ministries are in towns and villages along the borders. Also, each diocese receives a monthly institutional subsidy from the Government. An agreement signed with the Vatican in 1980 grants the Catholic Church special status in Peru. The Church receives preferential treatment in education, tax benefits, immigration of religious workers, and other areas, by the agreement. Roman Catholicism is considered the state religion of Peru.

Although the Constitution states that there is freedom of religion, the law mandates that all schools, public and private, impart religious education as part of the curriculum throughout the primary and secondary education process. Catholicism is the only religion taught in public schools. Besides, government buildings and public places have Catholic religious symbols. According to the 2017 Census, 76% of the population over the age of 12 identified themselves as Catholics.

Throughout history, it is not uncommon for people to attribute natural disasters as signs of God's displeasure with the inhabitants of the earth. Saint Francisco Solano's sermon in 1604 illustrates the long history of equating Lima's earthquakes with God's anger.

An Old Testament scripture often used to back up that claim is in Amos, Chapter 3:

2: You only I have known
Of all the families of the earth;
Therefore, I will punish you
For all your iniquities.

6: Shall a trumpet blown in the city
And the people not be afraid?
Shall there be evil in a city,
And the Lord hath not known it?

7: Surely the Lord God
Will do nothing,
But he revealeth his secret
Unto his servants, the prophets.

8: The lion hath roared,
Who will not fear?
The Lord God hath spoken,
Who can but prophesy?

After the earthquake in Lima in 1746, there was a decade of vigorous debate about what caused that quake. While some proposed natural causes for the calamity, the vast majority saw it as a sign of the wrath of God. They evoked and, in many cases, brought into the streets, the city's hallowed group of saints and religious images. The praying, processions, and nonstop masses in the days following the tragedy supported the observation that earthquakes were "collaborators with the Inquisition," as they persuaded almost everyone to decry the city's sinful ways. Guilt and fear about the prospect of further divine wrath due to Lima's immoral behavior paralyzed much of the population. Some took consolation, however, in the belief that if the people amended their errant ways, the punishment could be prevented.

Even in the 1960s, it was not surprising that in the small mountain town of Yungay, the native Catholic Priests would continue to use the same arguments, except to say that the people listening to LDS missionaries was the cause of the calamity. In 1965 the missionaries had been run out of town. After the earthquake in 1970, the missionaries in Caraz, which was close to Yungay, felt threatened enough to leave town as soon as they were able to obtain transportation.

On the other hand, in Huaraz, which was about ten times as big as Caraz, the Catholic Priests were North American. The Priests had a better relationship with the LDS missionaries and let them stay and eat with them after the earthquake.

After the 1970 disaster, the LDS missionaries and church members attributed their safety as a blessing from God, who was punishing the unbelief of the local people.

Chapter 3

Missions of the Church of Jesus Christ of Latter-day Saints

Missionaries of The Church of Jesus Christ of Latter-day Saints are volunteer representatives of the church who engage variously in proselytizing, church service, humanitarian aid, and community service. Missionaries are organized geographically into missions. Most areas of the world are within the boundaries of an LDS Church mission, whether or not any of the church's missionaries live or proselytize in the area. As of July 2018, there were 407 missions of the LDS Church. The LDS church is one of the most active modern practitioners of missionary work.

The first mission in Latin America was an attempt in the 1850s by Parley P. Pratt to preach in Chile. Parley P. Pratt, an apostle, his wife Phoebe Soper Pratt, and Elder Rufus C. Allen, were unsuccessful in establishing a foothold in Valparaiso, Chile, in 1851-1852.

The real advent of fully functioning missions in the United States, on a large and permanent scale, was the organization of the Southern States Mission, which was started in 1876 with Henry G. Boyle as president.

The establishment of the Church in South America began in Argentina when some German LDS families emigrated there in the 1920s and requested that missionaries and Church supplies be sent to Buenos Aires to help them build the Church among their families and friends.

In 1925, The Church of Jesus Christ of Latter-day Saints sent Melvin J. Ballard, an apostle; and Elders Rulon S. Wells, who spoke German, and Rey L. Pratt, who spoke Spanish, both of the Seventy, to open the South America Mission. Under assignment from President Heber J. Grant, on December 25, 1925, in Buenos Aires, these men dedicated the vast area of South America for the preaching of the gospel.

Speaking at a Sacrament meeting in Buenos Aires in 1926, Elder Ballard likened the Church's potential in South America to a strong, mighty oak growing from a tiny acorn. He said there would be thousands of members and many missions growing from the small beginnings of the Church there, and South America would become one of the strongest areas of the Church.

In early 1926, before returning to the United States, Elder Melvin J. Ballard visited Peru and was impressed that it was a good place to send missionaries. This event was the first official LDS contact with the people of Peru.

The Church moved into Brazil in 1928, also in answer to requests of LDS German emigrants living there. The first Latter-day Saints in Chile were North American miners who worked in the mining district in northern Chile. The first missionaries were sent there from Argentina in 1956, and in 1961 the church established the Chilean Mission. The Church moved into Uruguay from Argentina in 1944 and from Uruguay into Paraguay in 1948. The first missionaries were sent to Peru from Uruguay in 1956.

Although several members lived in Peru in the 1940s and possibly even earlier, it was not until July 8, 1956, that Elder Henry D. Moyle, of the Quorum of the Twelve Apostles, and Frank K. Parry, president of the Uruguay Mission, organized the first branch in Lima. Frederick S. Williams, former president of the South American and Uruguay missions, was called to be president of the branch, which began in his home. On November 1, 1959, Elder Harold B. Lee, then of the Quorum of the Twelve Apostles, organized the Andes Mission, which included Peru and Chile, and later Bolivia, Ecuador, Colombia, and Venezuela. Headquarters of the mission was in Lima. Two years later, Peru had twelve branches of the Church and more than a thousand members.

Although the work went slowly for many years, in the 1960s, a General Authority, Elder A. Theodore and his wife, Sister Marné Whittaker Tuttle, were located in South America to supervise missionary work. The first units were established in Bolivia in 1964, in Ecuador in 1965, and in Colombia and Venezuela in 1966. The Church created more missions in the early '70s, and there was one mission covering all of Peru.

In 1970, there were small branches of the church in Caraz and Huaraz. The leaders of the branches were missionaries. The Ward (a local congregation larger than a branch) in Chimbote was led by local leaders and supported by several missionaries.

The Church organized the Lima Peru Stake on February 22, 1970, with Roberto Vidal as president. It had six wards, three branches, and approximately 5,000 members.

Chapter 4

ADOBE CONSTRUCTION

ADOBE BLOCKS ARE one of the oldest and most widely used building materials in the world. The use of sun-dried bricks dates back to 8000 B.C. (Houben and Guillard, 1994). Adobe is a low-cost, readily available construction material manufactured by local communities with local resources. An adobe brick is a composite material made of earth mixed with water and organic material such as straw or dung. The soil composition typically contains sand, silt, and clay. The organic material is used to bind the brick together and allows the block to dry evenly, preventing cracking due to uneven shrinkage rates through the block.

They can be subsequently assembled, with the application of adobe mud to bond the individual bricks into a structure. There is no standard block size, with substantial variations over the years and in different regions of the world. In some areas a popular size measured 8 x 4 x 12 inches (20 x 10 x 30 centimeters,) weighing about 25 pounds (11 kilograms); another popular size is 10 x 4 x 14 inches (25 x 10 x 36 centimeters,) weighing about 35 pounds

(16 kilograms). The maximum sizes can reach up to 100 pounds (45 kilograms) because the adobe blocks above this weight become difficult to move.

Adobe structures are generally self-made because the construction practice is simple and does not require additional energy consumption. Skilled technicians (engineers and architects) are usually not involved.

In addition to its low cost and simple technology, adobe construction has other advantages, such as excellent thermal and acoustic properties. However, adobe structures are vulnerable to the effects of natural phenomena such as earthquakes, rain, and floods.

Because of the low cost, the use of adobe is widespread in developing countries. Unfortunately, many of those countries are also in some of the world's most hazard-prone regions: Latin America, Africa, the Indian subcontinent and other parts of Asia, the Middle East and Southern Europe.

Around 30% of the world's population lives in earth-made construction. Approximately 50% of the people in developing countries, including the majority of the rural population and at least 20% of the urban and suburban population, live in earthen dwellings (Houben and Guillard 1994). For example, in Peru, 60% of the houses are built of adobe or rammed earth.

During strong earthquakes, due to their heavy weight, these structures develop high levels of seismic forces which they are unable to resist, and therefore they fail abruptly. Typical modes of failure during earthquakes are severe cracking and disintegration of walls, separation of walls at the corners, and separation of roofs from the walls, which, in most cases, leads to collapse.

Although, since 1970, much work has been done by engineers to change the design of adobe structures to make them more earthquake resistant, considerable damage and loss of life have occurred in areas where people have used these materials. The reports from recent earthquakes confirm this. In the 2001 earthquakes in El Salvador, more than 200,000 adobe buildings were severely damaged or collapsed. 1,100 people died under the rubble of these buildings, and over 1,000,000 people were made homeless (USAID El Salvador 2001.) That same year, the earthquake in the south of Peru caused the death of 81 people, the destruction of almost 25,000 adobe houses, and the damage of another 36,000 dwellings, with the result that more than 220,000 people were left without shelter (USAID Peru 2001.)

Chapter 5

THE PEACE CORPS IN PERU

WHEN PRESIDENT KENNEDY signed the Executive Order to establish the Peace Corps in 1961, he sought to "encourage mutual understanding between Americans and people of other nations and cultures." Kennedy's words echoed in the ears of those who lived during a decade of social tension and Cold War anxieties and had a desire to make a better world.

The Peace Corps first opened a program in Peru in 1962. During the next 13 years, over 2,600 Volunteers worked in health and nutrition, city planning, social work, agricultural extension, agricultural cooperatives, savings and loan associations, elementary and secondary education, community development, and earthquake reconstruction (after the severe earthquake and landslide of 1970). Peace Corps Response sends experienced professionals to undertake short-term, high-impact service assignments and manages a response program that involves an annual placement of up to twenty, 12-month assignments. The Peru Response program also places volunteers in jobs focusing on cross-cutting development priorities in gender equality and working with people with disabilities.

Two Peace Corps Volunteers were killed in the 1970 earthquake: Marie Cluterbuck (22) and Gail Gross (23.) Gail worked in the Departamento de Agricultura. Peace Corps Volunteers assigned to agriculture programs worked on livestock projects, crop cultivation, and rural planning.

The Peace Corps had a central office in Lima and regional offices in Puno, Cusco, Chimbote, and Arequipa. The Peace Corps left Peru in 1975 due to political and economic instability but returned in 2002.

Chapter 6

EARTHQUAKES OF PERU

PERU IS A region of significant seismic activity, with as many as 200 minor earthquakes occurring on average each year. According to the Country Studies website, there have been more than 70 significant earthquakes in Peru since 1568, or on average once every six years.

The country is in an active seismic zone, so earthquakes are frequent. The interface between the Nazca and South American tectonic plates is located along and near the west coast of South America. Earthquakes occur as thrust faulting on the interface between the two plates, with the South American Plate moving towards the sea over the Nazca Plate at a rate of 77 mm (3.0 in) per year. The Nazca plate that lies in the eastern Pacific Ocean is pulled towards the South American continent. Due to the pull, it meets with the South American continental plate. The oceanic plate is denser, so it moves underneath the continental plate. Where the marine plate subsides into the mantle in the Earth's interior is called the subduction zone. The Atacama trench defines the boundary between the subducting Nazca plate and the South American plate. The same process has caused the continuing rise of the Andes mountain range and the creation of the Peru–Chile Trench as well as volcanism in the Peruvian highlands.

Peru's earthquake written historical references date back over 400 years to 1553. The first descriptive account of a shock tells of a "terremoto" that killed 30 people and destroyed much of Arequipa in 1582.

The deadliest earthquake in Peru's history before 1970 struck Lima in October 1746. A seismic sea wave (tsunami) which swept the coast killed at least 5,000 persons. Because of the Lima earthquake, there is still today an annual festival of "Señor de Los Milagros" (the Lord of Miracles) in Peru. The annual procession is the largest of its kind in Latin America, and one of the most prominent Catholic festivals in the world, with tens of thousands of the faithful taking part every year. The procession honors a 350-year-old image of a black Jesus painted by a black slave. The earthquake destroyed all but one wall of the church where it was located. It takes 2500 people to carry this two-ton block of masonry through the historic streets of Central Lima in a procession from the Las Nazarenas church to the church of Nuestra Señora de la Merced. The parade has flags, bunting, and bright colors, with most participants wearing purple, the traditional color of the Nazarene nuns who care for the image throughout the year. Some still observe the tradition of wearing purple for the entire month of October.

During the next 200 years, the most destructive shocks in Peru centered in and south of the Callao-Lima area, causing much damage in Camaná, Callao, Abancay, and Yanaoca.

On November 10, 1946, a magnitude 7.3 earthquake, centered in the same region of the May 1970 shock, generated landslides that demolished the town of Quiches (northeast of Chimbote) and severely damaged Conchucos and Mayas. An estimated 1,400 deaths resulted. A new break in the Quiches Fault occurred, which cuts across the Peruvian highlands among the Andes.

A moderate earthquake located directly under a city can create damage far out of proportion to its scientific significance. One happened in May 1950 in the Inca city of Cusco (in southern Peru), which sustained severe damage, while few other towns felt anything. An impressive result was the destruction of buildings constructed in recent centuries since the Spanish conquest. In contrast, the stone walls and doorways built by Inca artisans were nearly all intact, showing little or no effects of the earthquake. Since the Incas were known not to use mortar between stones in construction, this is even more remarkable. They skillfully fitted together great massive stone blocks in a secure, interlocking manner. The extreme damage in Cusco (about 63 percent of the buildings had to be reconstructed) was due to poor construction of adobe dwellings and to the thickness of alluvial gravels and degree of soil saturation.

In October 1966, also centered near the 1970 epicenter, one of the most substantial shocks occurred. Over 20,000 were homeless in Huacho, the most severely damaged village of the area. A religious festival (perhaps associated with that mentioned earlier, established in commemoration of the great Lima catastrophe in October 1746) was in progress in Callao at the time of this quake. Several died when some churches collapsed. Along the Pan American Highway, there were landslides and huge ground cracks developed, and over 2,000 houses sustained severe structural damage in Lima.

Landslides, ground fractures, and overturned trees also accompanied a magnitude of 6.9 tremor in northern Peru in June 1968. The quake killed forty-six persons in Moyobamba.

A modest magnitude earthquake, only slightly larger than that which devastated Cusco in 1950, swept through the Pariahuanca area of central Peru in October 1969. The shock destroyed 60 % of Comas village and razed Lampa and Chilifruta. Many landslides resulted from this tremor, which caused 136 fatalities.

Chapter 7

1970 ANCASH EARTHQUAKE

A ONE-MINUTE-LONG EARTHQUAKE can do as much damage as the Hiroshima atom bomb. It happened one Sunday afternoon in the spring on 31 May 1970, off the coast of Peru in the Pacific Ocean at 15:23:29 local time, while most were tuned in to the Italy-Brazil FIFA World Cup match. It began with a gentle tremor and began to snowball, expending its 45-second life in monstrous destruction, becoming the worst earthquake in the history of South America.

The undersea earthquake affected the Peruvian regions of Ancash and La Libertad. The epicenter was located 35 kilometers (22 mi) off the coast of Casma and Chimbote in the Pacific Ocean, where the South American Plate is subducting the Nazca Plate. It had a moment magnitude of 7.9 and maximum Mercalli intensity of VIII (*Severe*).

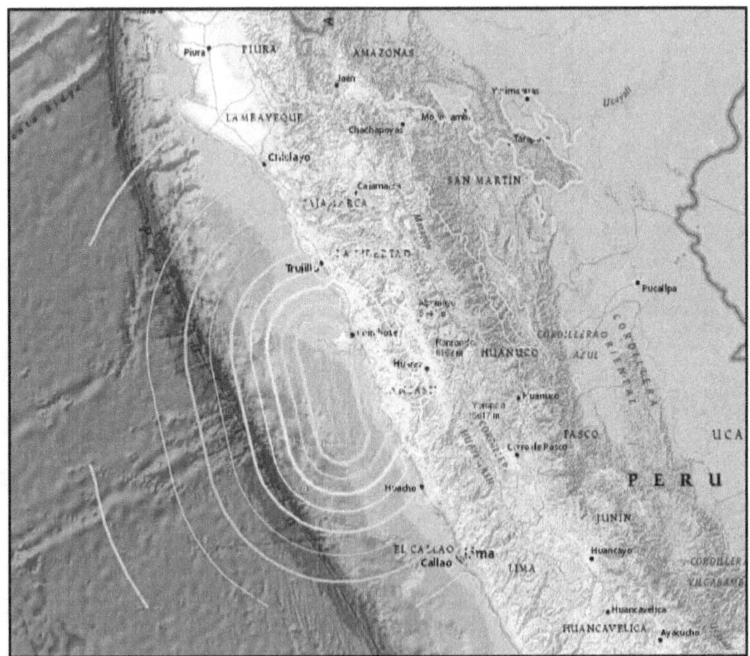

The motion knocked many off their feet when they escaped from buildings. Nothing could withstand the tremendous shaking of the earth. Houses, hospitals, deluxe tourist hotels, and apartment buildings crumbled like stacks of dominoes.

Roads disappeared, and dust clouds darkened the skies. The quake leveled towns and cities. Huaraz, Yungay, and Teofilo became rubble in seconds. An avalanche started on Mount Huascarán, a 22,20-foot ice-capped peak that buried Raurahirca and the remains of Yungay. In Chimbote, 55 miles west of Huascarán, 30,000 square miles was pulverized, and it resembled a bombed city.

Rescue work was attempted with bare hands because no tools were available. Thousands of injured died for lack of help. Because the quake knocked out communication, the world did not know the extent of the catastrophe for 48 hours. Information drifted

out by shortwave radio and early responders. Then help, food, and medical supplies began to arrive. But airdrops from helicopters smashed on impact, and whirring chopper blades started new avalanches.

There were reports of damage and casualties from Tumbes to Pisco and Iquitos in the east. In Ecuador, there were reports of damage and panic. Tremors from the quake were also felt in western and central Brazil.

It was a system-wide disaster, and the devastation impacted such a broad area that it disrupted the regional infrastructure of communications, commerce, and transportation. Economic losses surpassed half a billion US dollars. Cities, towns, villages, as well as homes, industries, public buildings, schools, electrical generation and distribution systems, water, sanitary, and communications facilities, were severely damaged or were destroyed.

Areas hard hit were the coastal towns and cities of Chimbote (the largest city in Ancash), Casma, Supe, and Huarmey. The Andean valley known as the Callejón de Huaylas suffered the most intense and sweeping damage, with the regional capital, Huaraz, as well as Caraz and Aija, being partially destroyed. Trujillo, the country's third-largest city, and Huarmey suffered minor damage.

In Yungay, a small highland town in the picturesque Callejón de Huaylas, the earthquake triggered an even greater calamity. The quake destabilized the glacier on the north face of Mount Huascarán, causing 10 million cubic meters (.35 billion cubic feet) of rock, ice, and snow to break away and tear down its slope at more than 193 kilometers (120 miles,) per hour.

NVDO. HUANDOY
ORIGEN DEL ALUD
LGNAS. LLANGANUCO
NVDOS. HUICHAJANCA
NVDO. CANCARAJA
MASHCA
RIO BUIN
MARCARA
MANCOS
CARHUAZ
RIO SANTA
YUNGAY
TINCO
RANRAHIRCA
QDA. STO. TORIBIO
N

INQUITUDE

Yungay. View looking east from Cemetery Hill showing village as it existed before May 31, 1970 earthquake and debris avalanche.

Yungay. The same picture after Huascaran debris avalanche.

As it thundered down toward Yungay and the town of Ranrahirca on the other side of the ridge, the wave of debris picked up more glacial deposits and began to spit out mud, dust, and boulders. By the time it reached the valley, barely three minutes later, the 914 meters (3,000 feet) wave was estimated to have consisted of about 80 million cubic meters (2.83 Billion cubic feet) of ice, mud, and rocks.

Within moments, what was Yungay and its 25,000 inhabitants were buried and crushed by the landslide. Many people died when they rushed to the church to pray after the earthquake struck. The smaller village of Ranrahirca was buried as well, the second time in a decade. But the image of lone surviving palm trees in the Yungay cemetery is burned into Peru's memory

Survivor Mateo Casaverde recalls, "We were on our way from Yungay to Caraz when the earthquake struck. When we stepped out of the car, the earthquake was almost over. Then we heard a deep, low rumble, something distinct from the noise an earthquake makes, but not too different. It came from the Huascarán. Then we saw, half-way between Yungay and the mountain, a giant cloud of dust. Part of the Huascarán was coming toward us. It was approximately 3:24 p.m. Where we were, the only place that offered us relative security, was the cemetery, built upon an artificial hill, like a pre-Inca tomb. We ran approximately 100 meters (328 feet) before we got to the cemetery. Once I reached the top, I turned to see Yungay. I could clearly see a giant wave of gray mud, about 60 meters (196 feet) high. Moments later, the landslide hit the cemetery, about five meters (16 feet) below our feet. The sky went dark because of all the dust, mostly from all of the destroyed homes. We turned to look, and Yungay, as well as its thousands of inhabitants, had completely disappeared."

In Yungay, only 350 people survived, including the few who were able to climb to the town's elevated step-like cemetery. The cemetery, which was built between 1892 and 1903, and designed by Swiss architect Arnoldo Ruska, who also died as a result of the landslide.

Among the survivors were 300 children, who were at the circus at the local stadium, which was on higher ground on the outskirts of the town. "The clown led the children to safety like the Pied Piper," Henri Gómez, a local tour guide, told the Peruvian Times. "As soon as the earthquake struck, he led them from his tent to higher ground."

About 80% to 90% of buildings were destroyed in Chimbote, Carhuaz, and Recuay, affecting nearly three million people.

The Pan-American highway was also damaged, which made the transportation of humanitarian aid to the region difficult. There was damage to the Cañón del Pato hydroelectricity generator on the Santa River, and the railway connecting Chimbote with the Santa Valley was left unusable on 60% of its route.

The world started to learn of the devastation of the earthquake on Monday.

Article from the New York Times

PERU ESTIMATES 30,000 DIED IN QUAKE THAT WIPED OUT SCORES OF TOWNS IN NORTH

Credit - The New York Times Archives

LIMA, Peru, June 1 — The Peruvian Government believes that more than 30,000 people were killed in the earthquake that devastated large areas of northern Peru yesterday.

The figure, which the military Government stressed was based on aerial surveys, was given to foreign embassies late this afternoon as sketchy reports from the affected regions filtered through broken communications lines to Lima.

Although the Government's estimate of the number of deaths was higher than earlier, nonofficial estimates, members of the international diplomatic community indicated that they were inclined to place credence in the Government figure.

Peruvian Air Force pilots surveying the valleys flooded by burst dams and buried under landslides radioed headquarters here that scores of communities "are no longer on the map." Whole valleys have become raging rivers and roads have been hidden by tons of rocks, they added.

In response to foreign ambassadors who asked for estimates of damage and offered relief services, the Peruvian President, Gen. Juan Velasco Alvarado, said: "We believe that at least 30,000 are gone, just based on estimates of the population in the areas surveyed by air today. We need help."

Amateur and mining company radio operators in the Andean areas today reported hundreds of deaths and devastating destruction. Among the hardest hit centers was Chimbote, a fishing and mining community where 200 were known dead and almost three-fourths of the flimsy houses destroyed. The epicenter of the earthquake was placed at 12 miles off Chimbote in the Pacific Ocean.

Peruvian military aircraft reported that the neighboring resort area of Huaraz had been leveled. Mining company stations said that at least 160 people were dead.

Here, in the capital, there were five known dead, four from heart attacks, and little damage. Some sections of the city were without lights as utility lines snapped. Communications by telephone and cable were broken. Roads north of Lima were blocked by landslides that affected many spots along the narrow coastal region to the Ecuadorian border.

The Government announced that the earthquake registered 7.75 on the Richter scale, the worst recorded here since May 24, 1940, when 200 were killed.

Chapter 8

~~~

MISSIONARY AND MEMBER EXPERIENCES

</div>

THE MISSION LEADERSHIP interviewed the effected missionaries as they came into Lima. The following account is taken from those interviews. The reports have been organized to conform to the timeline and lightly edited to improve readability. The missionaries in the affected areas played an important role in helping the members recover from the earthquake. Many of the missionaries were also able to help many other people get through the initial days after the quake.

Sunday, May 31

Lima

Though the tremors were the strongest that LDS Mission President Litster had felt in two years in Lima, most people had thought that they caused little damage. Late Sunday night sketchy reports of damage in the north along the Peruvian coast began to filter into Lima.
~~~

Caraz

Elder Arvig and Elder Nielsen described what happened in Caraz: Since it was the first of the month, we had decided to have a planning meeting, so we met with one of the Sisters in the second story of the Church to plan the Primary. We were just about done with the planning meeting, and I believe we had just had our prayer, when all of a sudden, the floor felt like it was going to fall out from under us. I suggested we get up in the windowsill. My companion noticed that the wall was wiggling, so he suggested that we go down to the patio. When we got down to the patio, we realized that four big walls surrounded us that all looked like they were going to fall on us. But to get out of the building, we had to go under an arched underpass, so we stayed there until the earthquake was over. At that time, we all knew that the Lord was really with us because the building truly should have fallen. Being a two-story building, it was a miracle that it didn't fall.

Elder Arvig continues: The earthquake lasted for about a minute, then we went out to the street. We couldn't see much because the dust had risen all around from all the houses falling, and you could see maybe three or four feet ahead of you. The sister that we were with started crying. She grabbed both our hands, and we started running up to her house to see if her mother was okay. As we were running, we had to climb over walls and different things that had fallen.

It seemed like every single person in the city was crying, and you knew that there were dead people all around you. Having been in Vietnam, I've seen families crying before, and I've seen little kids hurt before, but that was nothing like this because, in this case, there was nothing they could do. I felt inside at this time that we were extremely blessed. We went up to the house and couldn't find the sister's family, so we went up the mountain to look for them. Then we realized that the lake up above Caraz had most likely broken and was going to flood the city. So, we left this sister and ran back down to the city to warn the people and to try to get the people up to the mountains. The lake didn't break, but the lake down below us did, and because of this, I'm afraid that we did lose one or two of our members in the city of Yungay.

After they went to warn the people about the flood, the missionaries tried to unite the members and get them in the same place up on the hill. They then went down to the city once more, hoping to help the people. As they went down the street where they had walked so many times, the houses were in such a state that they couldn't tell them apart. When they got to the plaza, there were only four buildings that they could recognize. All they saw there were four injured people. The rest were either alive or buried. They saw one lady who had a bone sticking out and her foot, which was twisted entirely around the opposite way. She needed medicine badly, but they couldn't get the owner of the pharmacy to open his pharmacy to get any medication. They couldn't find any of the doctors in town. They looked for them but finally gave up hope. Later, when they went up on the mountains where the families were hiding, and the doctors were sitting with their families and not worrying about the other people.

The front part of the house the missionaries lived in fell completely. The room with their things held together reasonably well. They gathered together the blankets they had in the house and any other things they thought the members might be able to use. They spent the first night on the road under their blankets.

They felt good, though, as they went to bed that first night. While they were lying there trying to get some sleep, a man came up and talked to some people that were standing by them. He said, "The gringos are the only men in this town." Elder Arvig said: Although we hadn't done much, he made us want to try harder tomorrow." During the night, there were shaking and disturbances from the earth that woke them up, but luckily nothing happened.

Huaraz

Elder Kent Toone, President of the Huaraz Branch, and his companion, Elder Ladd Wilkins, were in Huaraz at the time of the earthquake. Elder Toone had been there for three months, and Elder Wilkins had been there for five months. Their account follows: We had a discussion set up for Friday, and as often happens, the discussion fell through. So, we set up another for Sunday at 3:00 p. m. At the discussion, we just got through the first conclusion when the phone rang. Senor Serapi Ortiz was talking on the phone when the ground started to shake. Elder Toone said I had been through two earthquakes in Ecuador, and so at first, I wasn't too alarmed. For the first five seconds, it seemed like it was quite a small earthquake. But then everything started to rumble like an approaching diesel train. I remember looking at my companion and telling him, "Let's get out of here!" We walked out of the gas station where we were giving the discussion, and the man, we were teaching followed us out in the street. It was a blessing, to be right where we were. That's one of the two streets that are still in existence in Huaraz. It is the widest street, and there are hardly any buildings on it. So, we walked, a minimum of about thirty yards. I remember starting to make a full turn to look at the things that were happening. I made just about half a turn when I saw the mountain to the southeast. It seemed like at least a half a mile of it fell off. A complete cliff fell loose. The dust that erupted from the falling dirt covered the city for three days. The helicopters that latter came with relief couldn't get in because they couldn't see where to land.

Elder Toon continues; Just about the time that I'd made a turn, it seemed like the earthquake was at its peak. The trembling was so great that I remember that I stumbled backward, and everyone in front, including my companion, fell towards me. It almost knocked us off our feet. The quake ended just after that, and the few buildings around us still had tile falling off the roof. The women were crying, and the children were running to where their mothers had run out to the middle of the street. It seemed like everyone forgot what they were doing. There was no one hurt around us, so the first thing we thought we should do was go to see the members. We started for the closest member who lived about two blocks from where we were giving the discussion. We took the other street that's still in existence in Huaraz to her street because the quake had completely clogged the streets with fallen houses. As we walked down that street, there was a part-member family that was standing out in the road. They're all girls, a whole family of girls, and they were hysterical. The house was still left standing, but they were in such a state of fright that they were crying and hanging on to one another. After a few seconds of comforting them and telling them that everything would be all right, we went on because we could see that none of them were hurt. As we made our way toward the member's house, there was a big crowd of people who were running around just trying to get out of the city. They'd lost their senses, weren't thinking rationally, and were running as long as they could run.

The street we were on is mainly a market street. There was one building a little bit down the street. The windows were broken out of that building, and the roof had fallen. At the time, during the earthquake, I didn't think that it was as bad as it was. The gas station where we gave the discussion just had a wall broken. As we started down the street Tarapacá, most of the buildings were cracking, and lots of them had fallen. So, as we got to the member's house, for the first time, I realized that the people were really in danger.

We saw this little member girl. Her mother was trapped inside the house, and she was standing in the door. She didn't know whether to leave her mother and run to get help or whether to try to dig her out herself. It was a good thing that we went to that house first. As we got to the door, we could see that there was one boy already taking adobes off the place where the mother was. I was a little bit scared for the lady. As soon as we got to where we could see her, we could see that her leg was trapped. This sister had her foot caught under a kerosene barrel. I was afraid her leg was broken. Otherwise, she was fine, except that she complained of sharp pain in her side. It took us 20-25 minutes to free her and an aunt who was with her. They'd been inside talking, and the member, Gudelia Quintana, had gone into the kitchen to fix something. At the moment of the earthquake, she'd run back in to get her aunt out of the house. It had taken long enough that they didn't get quite out of the house, so they stopped in the doorway, and that's why they were stuck.

After we freed her, we started around to visit the other members. Some of them lived in adobe houses, which I thought for sure had fallen in. They were the ones I wanted to visit first. We walked over by the hospital along Tarapacá and found out that Sister Vasquez had been seen and was okay. I'd been particularly concerned about her because she lived in a very old house. Another member, Brother Mallqui, a librarian in the town, had also been seen. We talked to him later. As we went up the street, we made a general loop, checking on members in the city. It seemed like we didn't run into too many of them that day because everyone was running around the city checking on everyone else, so no one was in their house. We asked the neighbors if they'd seen the person that we were looking for, and it always turned out that they had. We also were asking about our investigators. It seemed like everyone we asked about was okay; not one of them had been hurt.

The first afternoon we spent mainly walking around checking on people. We made one loop around the city. We couldn't go through the city because the inside streets were clogged with debris and adobe that had fallen. As we started to make our way up the hillside, we realized the extent of damage to the city. We went up the east side of the city onto the mountain. There was a new subdivision being built where we were going to start a school, and that was destroyed. There wasn't one building standing. Everything had just been leveled. We started into where some of our members lived, to see if they were there. This was the first time we had entered into a street that was clogged. We had to climb over rooftops and brick walls that virtually covered the street where we'd once walked.

As we walked around the city, the thing that I noticed was that everyone seemed to have been caught doing just what they were usually doing on Sunday. The cinemas were full. It seemed like every other person was drunk. Five or ten of these drunks came up and confronted us. They stepped right in front of us and asked. "What do you think about this misfortune from the Lord?"

The earthquake seemed to stop everybody right in what they were doing, just as it will at the Second Coming. I'm sure some of the members weren't planning to come to church that night and were going to go on a picnic or something. The first family that we saw, the Alberto family, was not dressed at all as you would expect them to be on Sunday. It was something to hear everybody talk about the "desgracia" (misfortune.)

Everyone, even the Catholics, were sure that the Lord was displeased with the way the people were acting. If we could have had a church service Sunday evening, or during the day on Monday or Tuesday, I know that every member, every investigator, anybody that believed in anything, would have come.

At about 6:30 p.m., we went by the church. We'd made the complete loop around the city and then decided the best thing to do would be to go to the chapel and see how it had faired. We walked past it because the blocks were completely unrecognizable. We finally recognized the church by its painted door. We walked over to the corner of the building where the offices had been. Elder Wilkin's office and my office were buried under more than ten feet of dirt and adobe. My desk was moved clear across the room with enough force to shatter one end of it. The two offices and every classroom were completely ruined, but the chapel itself was still intact. The roof was still above it. There were cracks in the wall, but nothing had fallen; the piano hadn't been scratched or the benches hurt in the least way. Also, the bathroom was okay, and the rooms adjacent to the chapel. It didn't seem like anything could be done there, so we went to our house. Our house was still standing, but the roof was very, very shaky. It was only balanced by a few bricks that were jarred loose. You could see cracks from the outside in the walls, and the bricks were leaning out, but the roof was still on.

It was getting dark, and the members around the city were in the same condition as we were, so we decided to get our clothes and blankets and take them to the members because the members didn't have anything. All of their houses had fallen while ours was left standing. There are small tremors that usually follow a quake, and while we were in that shaky house, it seems like the thought of that was most prevalent on my mind, because I didn't want to be caught there at the time. As we got everything out into the other room of our apartment and when we were ready to go down the stairs, both Elder Wilkins and I thought we felt a tremor, so we just left everything there and ran. But it turned out that it wasn't one, so we crept back up and took what we could. We were going to try to make it in one trip, so we put everything in a blanket. It was too heavy to carry, and so after trying to lift it, we left half of it there and just took two sacks of clothes and all the blankets we had. We thought they would be the things most usable for the people. It took us from about a quarter to seven until almost eight-thirty to travel four blocks over the rubble with the things we had in our arms. It took so long because it got dark, and the rubble was not beaten down.

All that my companion and I could think of then was that we wanted a drink. We went to the river. I thought it would be dirty, but I didn't know it would be as dirty as we found it. We dipped some up and could feel the mud right in our hands. As thirsty as we were, we thought it would be better to leave it. We went back to the gas station where we were when the earthquake started. Senor Ortiz still had water, so we asked him for a drink. It's amazing how our lives crossed with that man. I am sure that was one of the only places that had water that night

That night I told my companion I felt that we should go to the hospital rather than sleep. I knew something about first aid. We got a ride in the ambulance to the hospital and started working there. The condition in the hospital that night were the worst I've ever seen. My hands were filthy. I had washed them off in a muddy stream, but they didn't have anything else to clean up with that night, so I just continued working with my hands the way they were.

They didn't have any anesthetic to give to patients whose faces were slashed open. Some of them had their scalps peeled back from the back of their head clear to the forehead. It was terrible! They'd just let the people yell and scream while they sewed up what they could. The floor was like a butcher shop. The people were all muddy because the blood had wet the scalp, and the mud had stuck to it. And so, you cut the hair off and threw it on the floor. At the same time, there'd be gauze pads wet with blood on the floor. There was no time to clean up. There was nobody there to clean up.

I sewed up a few people. That's the first time I've ever done it. There were three doctors in Huaraz at the time, but they couldn't locate one of them until 11:00 p.m. or 11:30 p.m. that night, so there were only two in the hospital when we arrived. There were a few nurses. The only reason I started doing what I did was because one lady looked at what the others were doing and said, "You can't do any worse," so I sewed a few people up. The only thing they had to put on the wounds was streptomycin powder. It's usually given in an injection. You put sterilized water with it, and then you inject it into people as an antibiotic. But there was no water, so we used it dry.

I said to my companion, "the people we treat tonight will have a chance. They might have infections, they might be treated under the dirtiest circumstances, but a least they're having the bleeding stopped." There were people in the Plaza de Armas, but there was no way into it that whole night. One thing that was going through the minds of everybody in the hospital was that the theaters had been filled to overflowing, and all those people, the ones that were still alive, were in the plaza just bleeding and waiting for morning when somebody could get in and carry them out.

Elder Wilkins continues. I have a weak stomach, but from that first time Sunday night, I learned that weak stomachs don't do a thing for you. You have to forget about it because when something has to be done, you have to do it whether you have a weak stomach or not. I was standing there at the hospital Sunday night. We had all our stuff with us that we'd taken out of the house. We were carrying it around with us. There was a lot of robbing going on even Sunday night. My companion said, "Look, you just stand here for a minute and guard the stuff, and I'll get in there and start helping." I said, "that sounds like a pretty good idea, you know. I can stand here with my back to the wall and guard the stuff." Pretty soon, a German nurse came up and asked, "Are you hurt?" in English. I said, "Nope." And she said "Good! You can help!" So, they put me right in with my companion, sewing up people. Wow! It was terrible!

But, about 9:30 PM, some other men came into the hospital and said that they'd heard a voice down under the earth somewhere and they wanted some help to go get him out. So, I quickly volunteered for that. It sounded better than all the bloody people in the hospital. We went out a few blocks away from the hospital to dig out this little boy. When we first got there, we heard his voice under the ground, and it was so faint that they thought it would be impossible to dig him out; but we started digging. Everybody was still afraid of more earthquakes coming. We kept working and working and working! We didn't have shovels or picks or anything. All we had were our hands, so it was quite slow. We finally got the little boy out at 12:30 a.m. We couldn't see where he had been breathing from. He had been about six or eight feet under adobe bricks and dirt and rock, and he had not been able to move at all. We first found his hand. It was about an hour and a half before we could free him. When we got him out, he had a broken leg, and his face was all puffed up. There must have been thousands of people that were trapped like this little boy.

The thing that we commented on was that we'd found him: We'd dug him out: He was lucky. In some ways, people that were killed at once were the lucky ones because they did not have to suffer while they were buried. There must have been thousands of people that were trapped down there like this little boy. The buildings just fell from both sides on them. You could stand up on some points and look around, and it looked like a field of broken adobes. You couldn't tell one street from the other. The only way you could tell the street in many areas was by an extensive line of bent over street lights. There must have been a lot of people buried under there a long time before they died that nobody ever heard.

The Elders spent the night at the hospital. The hospital had electricity, but that was all. No water, nothing else. During the night, about 10:00 p.m., the ambulance quit bringing people. The doctors stopped and tried to get some sleep, and so did we. All that night, there were tremors. A couple of times during the night, the people in the hospital, even as hurt and badly in pain as they were, stood up and started to walk out.

Monday, June 1

Lima

By morning it was reported that Chimbote, where four missionaries were located, was seventy percent destroyed, with substantial damage in Trujillo, where another eight missionaries labored. Telephone and cable lines were down, and thieves began carrying off the downed wires. Communications were limited to ham radio operators and private company radios. Then Monday afternoon, urgent pleas started to come in through small private radios located in the Callejón de Huaylas, a narrow, deep valley located in Central Peru, over which towers Mount Huascarán, Peru's highest peak.

They reported ninety percent of the city of Huaraz destroyed, with the survivors of its thirty-five thousand inhabitants having fled in terror to the surrounding hillsides. Caraz, a city of twelve thousand, had reportedly disappeared from the map, being completely wiped out. The mission leadership's concern increased as they considered the two missionaries laboring in each of those cities and some one hundred Church members living there. Still no word from anywhere.

Monday night Dr. Alfredo Penarrieta, President of the Libertad District of the Church, called Lima on newly restored telephone lines from Trujillo. The district president found that 16 members of the Trujillo branch had been left homeless. He had been to Chimbote, and all the missionaries were safe. None of the one hundred seventy members had been seriously injured, though six families had lost their homes. Everyone was well in Trujillo. The chapel had not been damaged and was serving as a temporary shelter for several members who had lost their housing. Still, there was no word about the missionaries in the Callejón de Huaylas.

The mission borrowed a Volkswagen van from the local office of the Church Building Department. They began to organize a group to try to get into the Callejón de Huaylas to give aid to the members and to check the condition of the four missionaries.

Caraz

Elders Arvig and Nielsen continued their story: The second day, we piled our blankets up and went to the town once more trying to help. Unfortunately, the leaders of the town didn't accept our help. We offered many times, but there just wasn't too much we could do. They weren't organized, and they didn't want our help.

Luckily the first day, thanks to the quick thinking of one of the brothers, we were able to go to one of the stores and purchase some food for the members. The people had to go up the hill to get to the water to wash their dishes and wash their clothes and everything else. Most of the people had blankets, some of which they sewed together to make tents. Luckily the weather was nice. The days were warm, but the nights were cold.

Huaraz

Elders Toone and Wilkins continued their story: We worked at the hospital the next morning. All the nurses in the city came to the hospital that day. They started to bring in people at 6:00 a.m., and we left the hospital about 11:30 a.m. to go back to see the members because we had left them the day before as soon as we had found out that they were all right. We had found one member in the hospital. A brick wall had fallen on his arm, and he had been badly bruised and scratched up. The scratch wasn't very deep, so it didn't seem to be any cause for worry.

The first thing we tried to do for the members was to get them out and away from high walls and two-story buildings. There had been small earthquakes in the night, and I felt that as big as the first one had been, one half the size could come and the buildings as severely damaged as they were, could fall and kill a lot more people. We spent the rest of the day making sure people were moved out of that kind of dangerous situation.

That night we had our first meal since the earthquake. We were invited to eat with a member and her family where we had boarded. They were one of the families that we had helped move from their house.

Then we left and went up to the American Catholic Fathers' place. We had intended to do that even on Sunday night, so we could radio to Lima to tell them what we knew. It didn't seem like we had time. We got up there on Monday night and sent the message. The Catholic fathers said, "You can stay here, you know." We took them up on the bed that night because we'd given all our blankets to the hospital and the members. We each had a poncho, and that was all we had for the night. They told us that we could stay there as long as we wanted. They said, "You might as well eat right here." That evening when we came back, they said, "where have you been? We noticed that you haven't been eating with us." From then on, we started eating with them, and they fed us very well. During that time, I don't think the members or any of us ever went hungry. The Catholic Fathers were very good to us.

Tuesday, June 2

Lima

By Tuesday morning, the estimated death toll had climbed to five thousand, and our concern continued to mount. Still no communication from Caraz and Huaraz. The two dirt roads into the Callejón de Huaylas were both impassable. The highway from Lima to Chimbote was closed to all except official vehicles; no permits were being given. Finally, a Church member who worked in an appropriate government office called, and he could get us a pass.

The van was loaded with one hundred thirty blankets, three cases of medicines donated by another local Church member who headed a drug company, eight cases of canned milk, three cases of bread, and provisions for the five missionaries selected for the trip. The missionaries that were chosen to go were Elder Richard Fairbanks, who had been to both cities, Elder David Thompson, a professional builder, Elder Paul Newman, a former survival instructor, Sister Leslie Roberts, a registered nurse, and Sisters Mary Louise Riojas, a calm, capable lady missionary. They left Lima at 5:30 p.m. representing our only hope at that time for communication with the missionaries. Their instructions were to try to get an airlift into the Callejón de Huaylas as soon as the airport was repaired enough to permit landing there. They were to care for the injured and evacuate any injured missionaries. Realizing the grim nature of the situation, they also took burial clothing.

Elder Fairbanks said: We hadn't gone very far when I decided to turn on the radio to help us stay awake on the way up; we realized then that we didn't have a radio. We returned to the Mission Home to get a radio to listen to the news and any reports broadcast. We thought we might hear how to get into the Callejón after we got to Chimbote. Unfortunately, the radio we got wasn't any good, so we put it in the glove compartment and left it there.

We went rather slowly on the road. We couldn't go fast in some spots because the road was cracked and there were dips and bumps as a result of the earthquake. We were supposed to meet two Elders from Trujillo, and we didn't know who they were going to be in Casma that night at the bridge. But when we got to Casma about 11:30 p.m., there weren't any Elders. There were just some of the townspeople there. The town of Casma was completely wiped out; it was completely leveled. We talked to some people about how to get to Huaraz, and they said that we could go just a little bit up the road, and then we'd have to walk from there. They discouraged us and said it was out of the question because the road was completely out of condition.

Sister Roberts and Sister Riojas continues their account: We piled in the van and decided we'd head out to Chimbote and meet the missionaries there. After about two minutes of traveling, we heard someone yell "Elder," and we swerved off the side of the road. Sure enough, there were Elder's Gillespie and Fales in a taxi that they had hired from Trujillo to head out to meet us. Fortunately, they had received word from the Mission Home to meet us at Casma.

We jumped out of the car to shake hands and decided that we'd all go back to Chimbote and meet with the other missionaries. We arrived at about 12:30 a.m. and met some of the missionaries there. They were a little frightened to sleep in their own home, so they were in the Plaza Grande sleeping. It seemed a little ridiculous at first that they wouldn't sleep in their own home, but I sure know why now, after spending a couple of nights in Chimbote.

Elder Fairbanks continues: We went back to the communications center where they were going to try to call Lima to notify the President of our safe arrival. We had a contact from a company that is called the Corporación Peruana del Santa, which had a radio between Lima and Chimbote. We went there and talked to them, and within three minutes, we were on the phone, letting President know that we had arrived and what the situation was.

We hoped to possibly leave the next morning on a helicopter up to the Callejón.

Caraz

Elders Arvig and Nielsen continue their story: Tuesday night, we decided to go over and have our Mutual as on any other Tuesday, and we did so in our tent. We had our books there, and we were going to sing a few songs and have a prayer. As it came time to have the meeting, the people were in such a nervous state that we just ended up having prayer with them.

We passed Tuesday night reasonably well. The disturbances from the land continued, but luckily there was no panic or anything like it.

Huaraz

Elders Toone and Wilkins continue their story: In the morning, we left without breakfast and went down to see if we could move another member's family. We'd found them the day before while we were moving other members. We wanted to make a central location where we could have all the members camped where they could help each other.

It was a battle to get the people to move. We would say, "You'd better move out of your place." They would say, "This is all we have, you know, and we can't move." We spent the first few days trying to get them to a safe location.

The thing that I noticed most in the days after the earthquake, the idea that kept standing out, is that people after they got organized, dug stuff out of their houses. But the feeling that prevailed was they were just lost. They had lost their whole life. The people who had been there through the quake, who hadn't been hurt or shaken up at all, were walking around lost. They dug things out of their houses, just a chair or broken table, maybe a few pots and pans. I said, "What are you going to do with these things?" They weren't worth anything.

I'd say, "What do you expect to do, Brother after all this? Where are you going to go?" He'd say, "Probably to Lima." I would say,

"Do you have any money?" They would respond, "No." I would say, "How are you going to take your table and your chairs and all the stuff that you have here?" As you looked at, it was just junk, and everybody had it, but nothing worth anything. When you ask them, they'd realize it, and they'd say, "I can't take that. It's impossible. I couldn't get on a bus and take all this stuff with me." I'd say, "What are you going to do with it?" They'd say, "I'll sell it for whatever I can get out of it: Two soles or three soles ($1.00) is about it."

The day that we moved a sister out of her house, she had spent the night before, just sitting there. They didn't know what they were going to do. We went back the next afternoon and moved them out. The things she wanted to take with her were a chair, a table and pots, and pans. She was going to leave the food and the stove and everything else there. They were trying to hold onto the things that were, at one time, important to them.

There were planes over Huaraz on Tuesday morning, but they didn't drop anything. That was the first time we saw anything in the air.

Wednesday, June 3

Lima

At 2:00 a.m. Wednesday, Elder Fairbanks called by radio through the power company from Chimbote. They had arrived safely, but there was little hope of getting the group or the supplies into the Callejón de Huaylas. Perhaps there was a very remote possibility that one of them could get in on a helicopter the next morning if the helicopters could get in through the heavy overcast and the tremendous dust cloud raised by the earthquake and resulting landslides.

Just before Elder Fairbanks call, Elder Gordon B. Hinckley of the Council of the Twelve called from Rio de Janeiro, Brazil. He had left the Lima airport less than five minutes before the quake had hit the previous Sunday. Elder Hinckley asked about the missionaries, and when he learned that we had no word from the four in the Callejón de Huaylas, he advised us that he was going to come back to Lima. He said he didn't feel right about going back to Salt Lake City while there were still missionaries missing.

Wednesday morning, the estimated death toll had risen to thirty thousand, and there was still no word from the missionaries in Caraz and Huaraz. It began to look more and more unfavorable.

Caraz

Elders Arvig and Nielsen continue their story: Wednesday morning, we went with the people that were living near us in search of food. The way it is now, there are five camps where the people have gathered. They were called by a number, camps one through five. In the first camp are the town mayor, Catholic authorities, and the other uppity-ups, you might say, of the town. Camps two through five are for whoever happens to be there. If I remember right, we were in camp three.

As the time came to pass out food and distribute it, we noticed a significant difference in the way it was done. In our camp, we were very fortunate to have one of the city officials there with us. The first thing he did was go around to each tent, to find out the names of the people who were there, the ages, and the things that they'd need to stay alive and to be as comfortable as possible.

Once a day, a person in charge goes through a line and gets their portion of food. For example, my companion and I were just two people, so we'd get a ration for two people. The brother that we were living with and his wife had two babies, so they would get milk and things for the babies and any added supplies that they needed. And that's the way it went for the days that we were there. Fortunately for us, we ate well, but then we can contrast it with camp number one that had the mayor and the Catholic authorities. For one breakfast, they were eating beef steaks, drinking their wines, and things like this. Twenty yards away, people were starving; they would not give them anything to eat. They were sitting on the top of their food guarding it so no one would steal it. Some people were going without while other people were eating better than they'd ever eaten in their lives.

Wednesday morning, we realized that if we didn't get out of there, it might cause significant problems. People began to threaten us openly, so we then went to the airport to try to get out on a helicopter. However, the helicopters were transporting only the injured. We talked to a Lieutenant Colonel that flew in that day. He wasn't sure he could get us out; in fact, he said maybe we couldn't get out. But he said he would phone President Litster as soon as he got out.

Later, we went down to the airport again, and this time we were pleased because the co-piolet was a fellow whom Elder Arvig had known previously in El Salvador as a Marine Security Officer. How good it was to see his face! Considering we were old friends, I said, "How about a lift to Lima?" He replied, "Sure, hop on. Let's go!" We couldn't leave right then, so we told him that if we decided to leave, we'd see him Thursday morning.

That Wednesday afternoon, things started to get hot for the members and us. The people started saying that the Mormons were to blame and that we should be thrown out of the city. After the earthquake, after Yungay had been buried, the Catholic priest began murmuring against the missionaries, saying, "didn't we tell you that if you let them come back, the mountain would fall in on you?" The situation got pretty bad.

We had some excellent spiritual experiences too. We'd get together and talk about the scriptures. We had one of the brothers read from the Bible about the signs for the Second Coming of Christ. As we spoke, we felt the Spirit with us. They said that they never felt the Spirit as strong as they did in that tent. I can truthfully say that we knew that nothing was going to happen.

One of the Sisters asked us to lay our hands upon her head and give her a special blessing to give her courage and strength. I remember the feeling that I had filled my body. And at that time, I knew that the Lord indeed had preserved us and kept his Spirit with us. These people could kill us physically, but even if we died, we would know that once again we would be able to see our Father in Heaven in the flesh

Huaraz

Elders Toone and Wilkins continue their story: We decided we'd better go back to the church to see if we could get out the records and the money. We had been going to build a school in one of the neighborhoods with the money. We'd been having activities and had money from them in the Church. We were going to make a bank deposit with it, but it seemed like every time we had an activity, making a deposit got put off. It ended up that we were better off because we got the money and about half of the records. It was a job. We had to climb over the top of the building. There wasn't any ceiling or anything like that. Everything else had caved in except for the chapel. We climbed over the top of the wall at about 7:00 a.m. We started digging approximately where the desk had been. We dug clear to the floor but did not find the desk and almost gave up. Finally, we found a corner of the desk and got it out at about 1:00 p.m.

There was a helicopter that tried to land on Wednesday, but he couldn't, he said, because of the dust. There were also planes in the air that dropped things on Wednesday. That was the first time there were any relief supplies.

At about 3:00 p.m., they dropped the Prefecto, the chief magistrate, into Huaraz before they dropped a blanket or before they dropped any medicine. The man who had governed Ancash was killed in the quake, so before they dropped anything else, they dropped a guy so that they could get the paperwork done. The second thing that was dropped was the Sub-Prefecto.

Later there was a big DC-3 that came over and dropped medical supplies and a lot of men. Three doctors came in on that plane. Practically all the men came on Wednesday. There weren't a whole lot of supplies, but there were a lot of medicines and blankets.

We heard reports that they were still digging out live people. There were a lot of people who were down under there for a long time that died very slowly. I felt terrible for those people.

We were very dirty and exhausted, and we still had on the suits that we'd put on to go to Church Sunday morning. We looked terrible and felt worse. We went up the river and found a little bit of privacy and took a bath in the river and changed our clothes.

Continuing Sister Roberts account: At 6:00 a.m. Elder Fairbanks came running back to the van and said, "Come on, Sisters. We've got to get ready because we might be able to get up to Huaraz." We jumped out, and we started to put a few of our things together. We didn't know whether we could get in because I was a nurse or because we could be interpreters for the American people. We didn't have any idea of how we were going to get in; we just wanted to get in. The Elders even considered parachuting and just about everything else because we were so desperate to find the missionaries. It turned out that helicopters were just out of the question. They were booked up. There was a whole group of nurses and doctors waiting anxiously to get to the people to give them the medical attention they needed, and too many supplies that had to go, so we were right at the bottom of the list.

Elder Fairbanks wasn't going to stand for that, and so they headed out to find a guide, someone that could take them up the mountains.

Elder Fairbanks account continues: We decided we'd try to walk in, but we were a little bit hesitant, not knowing the way, not knowing the condition of the roads, and considering the possibility of postponed avalanches resulting from the earthquake. So, we wandered around trying to find somebody that knew the way there. Right off the bat, we were fortunate enough to run into a young boy who did. His name was Benjamin. He was sixteen years old, and he had grown up in the Callejón de Huaraz. His father was an old mountaineer guide who had taken many expeditions up on Huascarán. Benjamin seemed reasonably familiar with the area, and he had a pair of climbing boots on his feet. That's the first thing I noticed, and I thought he knew what he was doing because usually, you don't see a poor Peruvian boy who wears boots. The good English made boots. We told him the situation, and he offered to take us up there. He was excited about getting up there because he hadn't heard a word from his father or his aunt and uncle and family who were there.

Sister Roberts continues: Four of the Elders decided to go. Elder Fales and Elder Gillespie quickly changed their clothes and got themselves ready. Elder Newman, with this survival training, was one of the most qualified to go on the trip, along with Elder Fairbanks. So, the four of them and their young guide set out. Sister Riojas and I had a few doubts about it. We sounded like mother hens half the time, bringing up all the second thoughts about whether or not they should go. We prepared the food that they'd need for the couple of days it was going to take them to walk there.

Before we left we realized that we didn't have room for everybody in the van and all the gear that we had, so we stopped in Chimbote to leave some of the blankets and some of the food in our chapel, hoping that people wouldn't see it or break in and steal it.

About 12:30 p.m., we left Chimbote and went to Casma, and from Casma, we went the last forty navigable kilometers (25 miles) on a dirt road. We arrived at Yautan, a city which was also wiped out. We went through there fast. We took the red cross things off the van so the people wouldn't' think that we were there to help them and so that they wouldn't want all the food that we had. On our way, we got stopped by a man in another van. He was with the Peace Corp workers up there, and he was worried about them. The Elders took down their names and their descriptions and told him they'd do what they could.

When we got to the town, we saw the other Elders. We stopped, and the Elders told us that we had better get out of there because these people had not eaten at all, and if they saw us, they'd come after us because our van looked like it was full of food. So, we left town. We waited outside the town for a few minutes for the Elders to catch up with us, then we all went together to the foot of the mountain.

A couple of kilometers (1.2 miles) out of Yutan was where the road ended at a slide. The sister's account continues: Then we finished getting the Elders ready. They drank milk and got prepared to go. They took the tuna fish and most of the staple food for the long trek. So, at 2:10 p.m., the four Elders, with Benjamin as their guide, started walking along the roads where they could and where they couldn't, took short cuts across slides.

Elder Fairbanks continues: We walked until dark, which was about 8:00 p.m. that night. We kept walking even past dark until we couldn't see very well. Benjamin wanted to keep walking until 10:00 p.m. and get up at 3:00 a.m. Starting, we said, "Great, great, we'll do it. We're going to get there fast." We were going to walk that night to get to a place called Chac Chan, but the road was completely closed off. We couldn't get there because we couldn't see where we were going. It was late. To the right was a little footbridge that went across a fast, small river. The little footbridge didn't look very safe, especially in the dark. We decided we'd better walk back down the road where it was safer in case of an earthquake. Then, we were in a canyon that had big rock walls on both sides. About a half-mile back down the road from the bridge, we found a level area and part of the road that wasn't covered with rocks from a slide. We figured that was probably the best place to stay. We were too tired to walk farther down, where it was perfectly safe, so we just spent the night there. That night at about 11:30 p.m., things started to shake a little bit. We hopped up and nailed ourselves against the bank of the road, looking up to see if any rocks were coming over the top. Nothing happened. It was just a tremor; we went back to bed.

The Sisters continue: After the Elders left, we watched until we couldn't see them anymore, then we went back to town. We got to town about 5:00 p.m. We went back to the church and saw some more of the Elders that were there from Trujillo. Members of the church from Trujillo sent food for the members in Chimbote. We took some of the supplies out of the truck, and we put them into the house. The Elders went around, asking the members how much they lost and what they lost and made up packets of food and took it around to the members.

We got some soup going for the Elders because they had no food at all. We were eating when we heard a noise, and the house started to shake. We got out of the house. After we got out, the ground rumbled for a few minutes, and it stopped. We thought we'd better decide whether or not we were going to stay there that night or sleep in the Plaza. The church is about one-half mile from the ocean, so we could hear the ocean waves hitting against the shore. We had a prayer, and everybody felt that we should sleep in the Plaza. We loaded the car up with some blankets and food. We took it and went to the Plaza where we spent the night. We got settled down at 10 minutes after eleven, and another tremor came. We all stood up, and the ground rumbled and moved, and all the people went out of their houses crying and screaming. Afterward, we all settled down.

Lima

It was preparation day for the missionaries in Lima, and they streamed in and out of the office asking for news, almost afraid to hear the answers. Lists of the survivors and the dead were now beginning to come out of the Callejón de Huaylas and was relayed to the public through the Lima radio stations. Missionaries and members of the church were assigned to listen for news of the missionaries and hours dragged by with no news.

Radio messages were sent from Lima for the missionaries to contact the office in any way possible. A radio phone call came from Elder Richard Openshaw in Chimbote. The Elders were sleeping in the park. Elder Fairbanks, Elder Newman and two of the Mission President's assistants, Elder Richard Gillespie and Elder David Fales, who had been in the area when the quake occurred, had left early Wednesday morning with a guide to hike into Huaraz as there was no hope for going in by plane. They hoped to arrive there by Thursday evening. They only had to go fifty miles as the crow flies, but that distance was practically doubled by what was left of the winding road.

Frantic cries for help continued to stream from the Callejón de Huaylas. So far, the only support the people in the Callejón had received had come from thirty paratroopers who had jumped in on Tuesday afternoon. People were dying from simple injuries just because there was no one to take care of them. Aerial photos showed nothing but rubble and massive mudslides. Contacts were made again with personnel at the U.S. Embassy. Still, only official personnel were permitted on the flights between Lima and Chimbote, which had become the center for the rescue operations. We began to search for a trail bike that Lynn Gubler, Regional Supervisor for the Building Department, had offered to carry in as far as possible in his pickup and ride in on with a missionary. Somehow, we had to make contact with those missionaries! The feeling began to grow that they were injured and unable to communicate with the Mission Office. No one dared think about anything worse. A North American man who had left Huaraz the day before the earthquake called and reported that he had seen an aerial photo of Huaraz where the home in which the Elders had lived was absolute rubble. The hours dragged on. The lists of dead and survivors grew, but no familiar names.

Meanwhile, the missionaries in Lima began a fast for the success of the rescue group and the safety of the missionaries and the members in the Valley. Three days had passed without any news of them. Only two hours into the fast, the colonel who had flown the Elders into Caraz and to Chimbote called to report their safety.

At 9:30 p.m., seventy-eight hours after the quake hit, the telephone rang. "This is Colonel Beckett, U.S. Airforce. Would you like some word about some of your long-lost friends?" Would we! "Where do you think I saw them?" Caraz? Huaraz? "Caraz. How about some names?" Elder Michael Nielsen, Elder Allen Arvin? "Right. I flew a chopper in there today to study the possibilities for rebuilding the landing strip. They did some translating for me. They are well and happy, wondering if they could help more where they are or somewhere else." President Lister walked out of his office and shared the news with ten missionaries waiting in the outer office. Tears began to flow freely. Missionaries hugged each other. Some ran to tell others who remained in other parts of the building. Voices choked up. The tension began to ease. Maybe there was some hope now for the missionaries in Huaraz.

At 10:30 p.m., a cheer broke out in one of the upstairs offices where missionaries were huddled around a radio listening to reports from Huaraz. "Attention, Lima. Attention Lima. Mormon missionaries in Huaraz are well. We repeat, Mormon missionaries in Huaraz are well." The tears flowed again, more hugs, more scurrying to share the news. Elder Kent Toone and Elder Ladd Wilkins were safe. Grateful prayers welled up in the heart of each one of us. A call was placed quickly to the Missionary Committee in Salt Lake City by Sister Katherine Wright, and the good news was passed to them. All missionaries are now accounted for. The Lord has indeed been good.

At 11:30 p.m., the ground began to shake again. The window rattled, talking stopped, faces became taut again. Radios came back on. Where had this one hit?

Thursday, June 4

Caraz

Elders Arvig and Nielsen continue their story: That morning, when we came out of the tent, we had fashioned as a shelter, we found at the entrance a semicircle of candles, statues, and pictures that had been retrieved from the Catholic churches. Since in the mountains, a semicircle of candles in front of the door of a dwelling is a threat to the life of the owner, we went back to the airport hoping to get out. On the first trip to Chimbote, they made room for us and our baggage. There we met the Colonel we had talked to the day before. He promised us that once he got us out, anytime we wanted to get back, he would make sure we got back with all our equipment.

The arrangement was that he would take them from Caraz to Huaraz in his helicopter, and they could stay there overnight with the promise that he would take them out the next day. They were hoping to be able to find the Elders to see if they could help them.

The major had no alternative but to go to Huaraz to fuel because there was no fuel in Caraz. The Elders left a note with a man at the Huaraz airport for the Elders. The note told them what they were doing and asked them to get in touch with them in Lima as soon as they could. There was only enough fuel, so the piolet had to go straight over the mountains and down to Chimbote, so he took the Elders that day.

Yungay

The Elders from Caraz went to Yungay about once a week and visited the members there. They gave a few discussions and had some investigators. One brother and his wife, who was killed, had just for the first time come to the church about two weeks before. At first, they wouldn't even accept the missionaries in their house, but finally, they got them out to church. The missionaries did develop a feeling for this family, and it hurt them to seem them get killed. The two members had not been active in the church since 1965 when the missionaries had been run out of Yungay due to the influence and pressure of the Catholic priests. The priests had threatened the people that, among other things, the mountain was going to fall in on them if they didn't get the Mormons out of the city.

One group of non-Mormons came to the defense of the missionaries. In a local paper, these people published a statement in their defense, declared the right of the missionaries to be there, and their right for freedom of religion. They had signed their names to the article. Eventually, however, the missionaries left. During the days that followed the earthquake, in which more than 20,000 of 25,00 people in Yungay were killed, lists of survivors were broadcast from the stricken areas. One elder in Lima, looking through the mission history of Yungay, while monitoring the broadcasts for the names of the missionaries in these areas, told the mission president, "An interesting thing is happening. I was reading about these people who published their defense of the missionaries. These same names are coming out on the survivor lists from Yungay!"

Elders Arvig and Nielsen had flown over Yungay that day in the helicopter as they were leaving. They said it was just impossible to recognize the city. It looked like a big riverbed completely covered with mud. The only two things that they could recognize in the whole city were two palm trees that reached above the mud in the Plaza de Armas and the raised cemetery. They were told that, of all the city, there were only something like 170 or 180 people that escaped the mud and the water. As for the city itself, there were no buildings to be seen. The mud and the rocks had just covered it entirely over. Down below in the mud, you could see, once in a while, dead animals or people running, trying to find a safe place.

Chimbote

Sisters Roberts and Riojas account continues: We woke up this morning at 6:00 a.m. From then on, we sewed up all the blankets because they thought they were going to be thrown from a helicopter. After we got everything ready, we took it out to the airport. That's where we met the Elders from Caraz. We returned to Lima with the Elders in the Van.

Between Chimbote and Huaraz

Elder Gillespie continues: People started to come by about 3:00 a.m. saying, "All right children. Let's go! Everybody up." We were tired because we hadn't slept in Chimbote. We decided that since we had stopped because of the dark the night before, we'd wait until the sun came up to see how the bridge was. So, we got up about 5:00 a.m. and started moving around and had some milk and tomato juice and hot dogs. We ate it up! Then we went up to the bridge and went across it. It was quite sturdy. During the day, we crossed the river again higher up, and a couple of times, I almost fell in. There was just a log going across, and everybody was ok crossing it by straddling it. But I started walking across and fell over, but turned back and fell straddling the log, then crossed that way, like everyone else. I gave the others quite a scare.

We made quite good time. When one of us got tired, another one would take the lead. We soon passed everybody that had passed us at 3:00 a.m. We had a greater desire, I guess, or longer legs. At 10:30 a.m., we reached Chac Chan. The river was very clean there, so we stopped and talked to the people about routes from Chac Chan to Huaraz. We let our feet soak a little, and we washed. Then we started again, and that's when it first got difficult. We had to go straight up the side of a mountain. That was very hard. As our guide had been Lima, I thought he'd have a rough time too, but he just went right on up. That was only the first of the difficult parts.

Elder Fairbanks had to stop to rest, and he caught up with us after about fifteen minutes. We were up nearly eight thousand feet. We kept climbing up until we got on a good road. It was winding around the mountains, so we walked on a gentle incline. We went up the hill and stopped with an Indian family. They cooked us some corn and some mazamorra de zapallo (squash starch pudding), and it was terrible. Elder Newman kept telling us that we weren't in Lima, so we had to eat it. So, we took some of it with us.

Later we heard a helicopter. We tried to wave it down, but the pilot didn't come down, so we kept walking. Just as it was getting dark, we got to a rocky canyon. We hurried up and went through that. The road started making switchbacks, so we started cutting those. We got very tired. I guess Elder Fales and I were the ones who held up the group that night. We couldn't make it. We were getting higher; we could tell because our lungs ached and were burning up inside. The guide wanted to make it to the peak, which we made the next morning in about two hours. We knew we weren't going to make it that night, so we camped out on the road, right there, just a little bit out of the wind and by some water.

We had bread and some tomato juice and some canned milk, hot dogs, chocolate candy bars, and tuna fish. The tuna fish was what kept us going. It wasn't very heavy. We were going to take our sleeping bags, but Elder Newman said that they would be too heavy, so we just took a blanket apiece. We spread two blankets on the ground and two blankets on top of us and slept on the width of it. With four of us on the blankets, they came to about our chins, and our feet stuck out. It was freezing. Every time somebody would turn over, the one on the other end wouldn't have any blanket. We hardly slept all night. It was terrible. The guide had a sleeping bag. One of those nice warm ones

Huaraz

Elders Toone continues their story: We went back to the hospital and offered our services. I started giving typhoid shots. We spent the entire day giving about 150 shots. We went back up to where one of the members had moved and gave shots. It was difficult talking the members into getting shots. They would say something like, "We've heard that people are getting sick for a few hours from the shots. We don't want to get shots. We feel fine."

Two planes of supplies came on Thursday. That's when most of the things came. I think they even dropped some food on Thursday.

Two Peace Corp partners, two girls, were killed. They looked for their bodies in front of their house, and they couldn't find them. Finally, Thursday night, they found the spot where their bodies were.

Lima

Elder Gordon B. Hinckley was at the mission home, interviewing the missionaries that had been in the affected areas and accessing the needs of the members. Plans were discussed on what relief was needed and how to get that relief to the members. There was discussion about if the people in Caraz would accept assistance from the Church since the Elders had been threatened there. Elder Nielson said in Caraz that food of any kind would be very much in order; also, they need water, kerosene, cooking oil, and bread. Elder Hinckley was in contact with church headquarters coordinating the required supplies.

Friday, June 5

Caraz

The following is a translation of a letter received from Sister Elsa Ruth Alba; a member of the Caraz Branch written on June 5, 1970:

Dear President Litster:

I write you these lines to greet you, your wife, and the brothers and Sisters in Lima, at the same time thanking you for the thirty-one blankets that you generously sent to us, your brothers and Sisters in Caraz, who find ourselves in difficult circumstances. I thank you on behalf of all of the members and hope our Heavenly Father will bless you richly.

Personally, Brother Litster, I am very, very grateful to my dear Heavenly Father for the goodness and mercy that he has shown and does show toward me and toward all my family and towards the members of the Caraz Branch. He has saved us from dying among the ruins; my testimony of the truthfulness of our Church grows because, in these critical moments, my Heavenly Father has given us and continues to give us more spiritual strength. Difficult and sad have been these tragic moments, but the Spirit of the Lord is and has been with us to protect us. Truly, the city of Caraz is in ruins except for a few homes that are still standing but badly cracked. Our dear meeting house has not been so totally affected; we hope to be able to have Sunday School this Sunday in the patio as well as testimony meeting. It is marvelous, brother that I can feel the Spirit of the Lord during my prayers in these tragic days as I do at this moment with such fervor that it causes me to shed tears. Oh, my brother, I have no doubt that God the Father and Jesus Christ live and that we are in their True Church. The members and missionaries have not even received a scratch because of the earthquake. Elders Nielsen and Arvig went to Huaraz in a helicopter to look for the other Elders. We are worried because we know nothing about them, but we trust in God that they are alive and well.

Truly, my brother, I think that the Callejón has been chastised for not having accepted the message of the Church of Jesus Christ due to the idolatry of the people. I know that

Huaraz is going to be burned, perhaps Caruhas as well. Yungay has totally disappeared, while in Caraz, though, in ruins, the major part of its inhabitants has been saved. Yesterday we had a public meeting and all the people are optimistic about reconstructing the city of Caraz. All the men fifteen years old and above get together in large battalions with their shovels picks and crowbars in order to construct within a few days another landing strip and thus be able to receive greater help and thus get out of the desperate state in which we find ourselves. I have cried a great deal as I see the city in ruin, but I have confidence and faith in our Heavenly Father, that He is preparing something important for the progress of His Kingdom on earth. I also hope with all my heart that this test the Lord has sent us will not cause the Caraz Branch to be closed but rather, as were planning Sunday with the Elders in the monthly Primary preparation meeting just minutes before the earthquake, we are committed to teach the message of the Primary of the Church of Jesus Christ to the lame, the blind, the poor, now that the chosen ones have rejected it.

Brother Lister, I would be the saddest person on earth if our dear Caraz Branch were closed. It is certain that the people here are very, very hard, but I am sure that there are many people who have an open heart, though their traditions and prejudices such as "what will the people say?" prohibit them from accepting the gospel and being members of the True Church. The Elders have worked hard, but I think, brother, that in Caraz one must struggle with the very forces of the devil who is here in strength. Nevertheless, I am sure that the forces of Jesus Christ are stronger and I believe that the enders and members should not be weak at any moment.

I should tell you that all the survivors from the city of Caraz are living in tents made of blankets, others from branches. Thus far, with the blessing of our Heavenly Father, we are not yet suffering hunger because we receive indispensable daily food rations. The government is sending help in medicines, foods, etc. but it is arriving in small quantities because the helicopters will carry very little. We are now calmer, and I have great faith in our Heavenly Father that within a short while, things will be better. I plead with you to pray for us so that no epidemic may break out among us and so that Lake Paron may not break and spillover.

With all the love of the gospel,

Your sister,

Elsa Ruth Alba R.

P.S. Many affectionate greetings from the members of the Caraz Branch. Though we are afflicted, we have the Spirit of the Lord to console us. The members are saddened because of the loss of one of the unbaptized daughters of Sister Barrios. They plan to go to Lima. The Ramirez family is also intending to go to Chimbote. I intend to stay here because of my work.

Huaraz

Elders Toone and Wilkins continue their story: Friday morning, we went with the Peace Corp guys to help them dig out the girls. That was a terrible experience for us. But you learn a lot even from bad experiences. After being buried from Sunday until

Friday, the bodies were decomposed. The only way you could tell them apart was that one of the girls had long hair, and the other girl had short hair, and we could tell a little bit by their clothing. The Peace Corp girls had their arms wrapped around each other. We tried to think of a way to get their bodies out of the city. The helicopters were coming in then, but they were taking out the sick ones. Also, the bodies were so decomposed that we finally decide we'd better bury them right there. We took them up to the Catholic fathers and buried them on their grounds. We had to put the bodies in a plastic bag and bury them that way. We were really good friends with the people in the Peace Corp. One of the girls was Catholic, and the other one was Lutheran. The boy who was the local head of the Peace Corp there consented that one of the fathers from Los Pinos say something over the grave. We took their things and sent them to their parents so that at least their parents would know that they were found and that they were properly buried.

One brother of a member family that we had moved out of a second story building was the owner of a store. They moved in with four other families, and they weren't boiling the water. They were next to the hospital. We thought that there might be a lot of typhoid; they were starting to give injections for typhoid that day. So, we moved that family again from near the hospital to a little meadow about half a mile up in the hills near where we were staying. There they were away from people and where water was being distributed. They'd bring it around in a big gasoline truck. We visited all the members and told them to boil their water.

The Odar family, the owners of the store, had brought all their food and their clothing when they had moved out. They'd faired pretty well. They'd only had one grandmother killed, and their store had been left intact. All the noodles and dry goods that they had were there. All their canned goods, like milk and canned tuna, had come through all right. I thought that if we could get the members there, Brother Odar had enough food to help them out if any of them lacked anything. But he'd been so open-hearted that he'd given it to a lot of his neighbors. He distributed all the food that he had to them. All he had when we talked to him when he moved up to the meadow was just rice, some milk, and a few other dry goods. They didn't have any meat or fresh food of any kind.

Friday, when we were about to eat lunch at the Catholic Fathers home, Brother Odar came up with a lot of stuff in a truck and began looking for a place to make camp, so I went out to help him for a minute, then I went back to eat. I'll never forget how confused I was when I saw the four Elders standing there when I returned. From the time I saw them until I got up to them, I had my hand in front of me ready to shake their hands, but my mind was thinking. "Now, how in the heck; there's no way to get in here." I didn't know whether I was dreaming or what, but they were a welcome sight. We had felt like we were the only Mormons in the whole world up there for a while, and it was good to see them. Even if they didn't do anything else, they changed our mental attitude and made us feel a whole lot better.

Elder Gillespie continues: I think that the most significant local relief problem was the lack of organization. Even when we got there on Friday, they were flying around in a circle above the town, pushing things out. The heavy stuff was dropped with parachutes, but the blankets were just dropped by themselves. On Friday and Saturday, we heard the officers talking about the lack of organization. One fellow said, "Yes, we're trying to get things organized." They might have had quite a bit there, but it wasn't being distributed, at least not very effectively.

Elder Fairbanks continues: Another problem was trying to coordinate the different armed forces. The Peruvian with the American with the French, and I believe with even Japanese and English. They weren't organized in any way. That's one of the things the Americans were complaining about. Each was trying to do it on their own.

Friday night, when we finally did get into radio contact with the mission office in Lima. On the call, we commented that even though everybody around the radio was making noise while we were talking, it was a thrill to year President Litster and Apostle Hinckley's voices. Everything quieted, and you could feel the Spirit right there with us. It was a thrill to finally make contact with the rest of the Church and with the rest of the world.

Between Chimbote and Huaraz

Elder Gillespie continues: At 3:00 a.m., people came by again waking us up, the same ones that woke us up the morning before. So, we got up about 5:00 and started hiking. It was hard, but we finally made it up to the peak, which was around fourteen thousand feet. It was pretty hard going that high from sea level.

We walked through a few towns, and they told us that some people were dying from the altitude. I didn't think very much about it until I tried to go over the top. The guide got upset with me, grabbed my hand, and pulled to help me. Finally, I had to take a rest. He let go, and I fell, and I was out.

Elder Newman continues. Friday morning, it took us from 6:00 a.m. until about 9:00 a.m. to get to the point. We sat down but didn't rest there very long, just long enough to realize that we had made it to the top. That gave us a thrill and got us ready to go down. It was another two or two and a half hours from there to the city.

It was all downhill, so we went pretty fast. We stopped once and got water and rested a little bit and then went right on down the mountain into the city. Every once in awhile, we'd run into people who were walking out from Huaraz. We asked them about the gringos up there, if they were all right. We heard good reports from everyone that they were well and that they were helping, many said, in the hospital.

Upon entering the city, we left our guide with his family, and wonderfully enough, they were all fine. He hadn't lost anyone in his family. The Lord blessed him in that. On the trail, we had been talking some about the Gospel. I believe that he plans to meet with some missionaries again sometime. He was very interested in the things that we believed. Maybe he'll hear the lessons. We entered the city about 11:30 a.m. and immediately began asking for the Elders, trying to find out where they were.

Elder Fairbanks continues: When we arrived in Huaraz, we heard that the Elders were in the hospital helping out. The word had spread around town about the Elders. The first place we went to when we got into town was the hospital. We walked right in the past a check-in because we were Americans. We saw some men from the special forces, from the Green Berets. We started talking to them, and they were very helpful to us. They had come in by helicopter and were there with aid. They gave us some "K" rations; we had beef, potatoes, and ham and eggs in little cans. It probably wasn't very good for you, but it sure tasted good. It was better than buttered bread. They also gave us vaccinations against typhoid. One of them had been in Caraz the day before, and he told us that he had seen and talked with the Elders there. He said to us that the Elders were fine. The only problem being that the people were superstitious and were just a little bit mad at them and blamed the earthquake on them.

We kept hearing about Los Pinos. We knew that there was a radio up there, so we headed that way. Before we started in that direction, we looked around the city a bit. The streets and the houses were all on the same level. Hardly any buildings we could see were standing except about a half a mile out of the city.

Elder Fales' feet were really in bad shape. His whole right heel was like hamburger. Elder Newman and I started for Los Pinos to try to find the Elders, and Elder Gillespie stayed with Elder Fales. We walked through the center of town to where the Plaza de Armas was. The street and the houses were on the same level. It wasn't so much that the houses were down to the street as it was that the street was filled up to the homes. We thought that we were never going to get there that way because we were hiking up and down over rubble and going too slowly. As it happened, we ran into Benjamin again in the plaza, and he took us on Tarapacá, one of the better-preserved roads. We met a special forces man driving along, and he asked us where we were headed. We told him that we were going to Los Pino to find the Elders. He said, "Hop in. I'll take you up." Instead of taking us directly there, he went back to the hospital. Since he had a truck, we loaded Elder Fales into it, and we all hopped in the truck. From there, we went back around the city to go up to Los Pinos. We arrived there just in time for lunch.

Elder Fales continues: We were very comfortable at the Catholic seminary. Sunday, just before the quake, they had brought their food for the whole week. It was paradise after what we had been through, and it was wonderful to be in a nice bed that night. I could hardly walk, so I just stayed there most of the time while the other Elders were getting everything going. After we were there for a little bit, Elder Fairbanks, Elder Newman, and I went down to the river and had a bath. It was nice. It sure felt good but was kind of cold.

I was talking to a man who was living there, a man about twenty-eight years old who was a mountain climber from San Diego. After the earthquake, he was trying to find his friends, and he'd hear people screaming under the piles of dirt. It was tough for him to walk past them to find his friends. He couldn't see them, but he could hear their screams for help. Also, he told me about a Peruvian girl he knew who was in a showhouse when the building caved in. She was one of the few that were saved. The whole ceiling fell in and opened up in the middle. The roof fell, and everybody all around her was killed and buried under it, but she stayed alive. She climbed out of the roof and said it was a terrifying experience.

The experiences of a lot of people in the town were so tragic that they couldn't process it. I was with Elder Toone downtown, and we met a lady and said, "Hi, how are you, sister?" She said, "Oh fine,"; then she broke down and shed about three tears and said that her daughter had died. Later on, as we were going out of town, when we ask another fellow how he was, he said, "Oh, just great. I lost a sister, but that's all." There wasn't time for any mourning. The situation didn't yet seem real to them.

Elder Newman continues: I would like to interject a small comment. In comparing the experience of the two and a half days that these Elders and I hiked into Huaraz with some lessons, I've had on survival training, taking students from Brigham Young University for twenty-six days at a time, going days without food and water and through some pretty severe experiences. I want to give tribute these Elders by saying that in those two- and one-half days, they endured physically as severe and as painful experiences as one has in twenty-six days living off the land without any sleeping equipment or blankets or anything and any stored food or water for as long as a month. So, you can see that they went through some pretty hard experiences. I remember looking back when Elder Gillespie was coming up over the point and seeing him faint on the trail. I remember seeing when Elder Fales pulled his boot off, and his entire heel was a blister. As far as justification for that goes, I would like to interject this also: Beyond concern that was felt for the Elders in Huaraz and the members there, there is a quality in great people that moves them to act upon situations. It seems like the more difficult or dangerous the situation is, the more they like it. It seems like often people will ask, "Why? Why this? or Why that?" And then there are those uncommon few who will always say, "Why not?" These Elders were that type of people. It's a quality that moves men to act upon situations, to face them fearlessly, to experience things that make men old and wise at the age of twenty or twenty-five. Still, it strengthens people and makes them grow, and I was proud to be a part of that company and proud to endure that experience with them. As long as they keep that quality and are never afraid to make efforts, they'll have some tremendous skills and continue to grow and be leaders for good in the Church and the world.

Saturday, June 6

Huaraz

Elder Wilkins continues: We went back to the hospital several times to see if we could help. When we walked in after the additional nurses and doctors arrived, it looked like a completely different hospital. We mentioned how filthy the emergency room had been; as soon as they got help, they completely changed that. They opened up other wings of the hospital they had not used because they had been afraid that these wings would fall in if there were another earthquake. They had all kinds of help and all kinds of medicine, and everything was a lot cleaner.

Saturday, we checked on transportation out. We had high hopes of a helicopter coming in and picking us up and taking us out. It took us about ten minutes Saturday morning to eliminate that thought from our mind. The next idea was to find some horses. About the only way that we could figure to get out was to get horses to take us up the peak of the mountain, and then we would walk down the other side. Of course, the Elders that had just walked in weren't very excited about that at all. But we didn't know how else we were going to get out. We finally heard word that the road to Huánuco was open, so we talked to some authorities there about getting out on this road. They told us that they'd permit us if we could find a car. But we couldn't find anybody that wanted to take their car over the road.

Sunday, June 7

Huaraz

Elder Wilkins continues: When we told the members that we were planning on having a Sacrament meeting and told them where we were going to have it, some of them gave us the same old excuses that they had given for months and months. They said that they didn't have time or that they'd be busy, or that they didn't know if they could come, but that they'd try as hard as they could to come.

On Sunday morning we had our meeting at 8:30 a.m. We still had a problem with attendance. It will take more than an earthquake,

I tell you, to get the members out to church. We started the meeting at about 9:00 a.m. with three or four members present. Most people got there about 10:00 a.m. It is typical of Peruvians always to be late! We held the one meeting out in a little wooded area up by Los Pinos in a nice peaceful spot. The two assistants to President Litster talked, and we had the sacrament, and oh, it was nice to have another meeting again! We were hoping that all of our members and investigators and everyone would be there. But even after all the blessings they'd received compared to the rest of the people, only about fifteen were there.

Monday, June 8

Huaraz

Elders Toone and Wilkins continues their story: We finally heard Sunday night that a bus was leaving on Monday morning. It was supposed to go at 9:30 a.m. We finally got all of us, including the Elders that had walked in, on the bus by noon.

Elder Fales continues: We went through some very, very beautiful Peruvian countryside. It was gorgeous going through high, snow-capped mountains, and beautiful open grass plains with cattle and horses grazing on then. The area was so remote that missionaries don't generally see that area in Peru. It was quite enjoyable, except for the uncomfortable condition on the bus.

There were beautiful rivers, mountain streams, and lakes between Huaraz and Huánuco. That part of the trip took us twenty-four hours

Tuesday, June 9

Huaraz to Lima

Elder Fales continues: When we got to Huánuco, we decided that we couldn't go on that bus any longer. It was just a little Ford truck with a bus on it. It was a kind of made-over vehicle. We decided to get a car which we did. We wanted to get back as soon as possible because we felt the people in Lima were probably worried about us, and we also felt a need to get back to civilization again. We got a rented car in Huánuco, and it seemed as if things kept going against us. Right outside of Huánuco, the driver pulled into another car and made a gash in the side of it. We kept going, and we had another little accident; then, we got into Lima and had a flat tire. We were all very sick and had headaches. Three or four of us threw up quite a bit. It was an experience we'll never forget, but it was terrific to get back to the mission office.

Chapter 9

Aftermath

THE ESTIMATES OF destruction and damages from the May 1970 earthquake vary but, suffice it to say, were enormous. For example, Carey (2005) suggested that the quake killed 70,000 Peruvians and triggered an avalanche from Mt. Huascarán that killed 18,000 people. On the other hand, Oliver-Smith (1999, 84) summarized the devastation in the region thus:

> The earthquake affected an area of about 83,000 square kilometers (32,046 square miles) or an area larger than Belgium and Holland combined. It claimed approximately 70,000 lives, injured 140,000 people, and destroyed or damaged more than 160,000 buildings, roughly 80 percent of the structures in the area. Over 500,000 people were left homeless, and the lives of approximately three million others were affected. Economic losses surpassed half a billion dollars. One hundred and fifty-two provincial cities and towns and over fifteen hundred peasant villages were severely damaged or destroyed. Also, home,

industries, public buildings, roads, railroads, bridges, schools, electrical, water, sanitary, and communications facilities were destroyed or severely damaged. The forty-five seconds of the earthquake obliterated much of the fragile material infrastructure of this large region.

This devastating event has also prompted Frommer (2008, 157) to state:

> While aid flooded in from around the world, and Peru sent in its military to keep the peace and try to get the most drastically affected communities back on their feet, it will take years for them to recover, and many who lost their homes [e.g., more than 37,000 homes were destroyed] may never be able to rebuild.

The missionaries credited their safety to the protection of the Lord. The following summary is from the Introduction in the booklet Earthquake:

Now, of the miraculous happenings of which there are many, one of the most interesting was the way the Lord's hand sustained the Saints despite the many, many people who were killed. There were 170 members in Chimbote, 85 other members in the Callejón de Huaylas. Over 900 members in Trujillo. Yet, despite all the destruction, there were only two members that lost their lives, and two others that were injured, a man in Chimbote suffered a broken leg, and a man in Huaraz had a badly scratched arm. The two members who died had lived in the city of Yungay and are believed to have been buried in the mudslide that followed the earthquake.

The Lord's hand was made manifest in every part of the affected area. The building that we used in Caraz was one of the few left mostly intact. There were cracks in the walls, and one could see daylight in the corners, but the building was standing. In Huaraz, the building was destroyed except for the chapel where the piano, pulpit, sacrament table, benches, and things like that were. Although all the rest of the building was laid flat, we even had to dig the records out from under eight feet of adobe, and the significant furnishings were not scratched.

The only damage to the building in Chimbote was a piece of ceiling plaster about eighteen inches square that fell. A wall from the building next door fell against a window of the chapel and just slid down the side, not breaking a thing. Across the street, a two-story reinforced concrete school was all buckled and twisted.

In Trujillo, where ten percent of the buildings were destroyed, and twenty percent more were damaged, our chapel wasn't hurt.

Many of the streets in Huaraz are so narrow that the wheels of a car rub both curbs. At the time of the earthquake, the missionaries were teaching a man on one of the two streets in all of the city that was not later filled with eight to ten feet of debris, mostly bricks and cement that fell. The house where the Elders lived was destroyed except for their room, which was left intact.

The two missionaries that were in Huaraz explained how they thought that the Lord protected them:

Elder Toone said: I want to say that the reason we're here, I know, is because the Lord took care of us. If we had been in our house, even though it didn't fall, we would have been killed because I'm sure that if we had been on the second story when we felt that earthquake, we wouldn't have been in the house very long. And if we had run out into the streets, as narrow as those streets are in Huaraz, we would have been buried just like the Peace Corp girls, under two layers of adobe brick walls. If we had been in the church, as we had planned to be, in our offices working that afternoon, there wouldn't have been a hope, as deeply buried as those offices were. Even if we had run out of the chapel, the chapel street was the same way, buried under eight to ten feet of adobe bricks. Each adobe brick weighed more than forty pounds, so you can imagine what it would have been like. That we were giving a discussion on the widest street in Huaraz where there were almost no buildings, at 3:00 p.m. on Sunday, is a testimony to me that the Lord was watching over us.

Elder Wilkins said: I think having the members saved the way they were was another testimony. Almost everyone we talked to had someone who had died in their families. Some of the families had lost eight to ten people. Some parents had lost all of their children, and we saw quite a few little children without homes. But every one of the members and investigators and their families was spared. They lost their houses and their things, but every one of them was fine. The Lord did preserve them, even though a lot of them had been inactive for a long time. They were members and had been baptized, and I'm sure the Lord protected them. They knew it too. We talked to many of them, and even the investigators bore their testimony the Lord had saved their lives.

The Epilogue in the booklet Earthquake:

We hope that this book has brought those who read it closer to the event itself and the magnitude of it. The significance of the earthquake for the members of the Church of Jesus Christ of Latter-day Saints is far greater than just another happening in the course of nature. The prophets of old saw these, the last days. Nephi spoke of these times 550 years before Christ:

But, behold, in the last days, or in the days of the Gentiles--
yea, behold all the nations of the Gentiles and also the
Jews, both those who shall come upon this land and those
who shall be upon other lands, yea, even upon all the lands
of the earth, behold, they will be drunken with iniquity
and all manner of abominations--

And when that day shall come, they shall be visited of the
Lord of Hosts, with thunder and with earthquake, and
with a great noise, and with storm, and with tempest, and
with the flame of devouring fire. (2 Nephi 27:1,2)

We recognize the proximity of the Second Coming of the Lord
and bear witness that these signs of the times reflect just that.

Sources:

Earthquake Information Bulletin, September – October 1970, Volume 2, Number 5

The Booklet "Earthquake" prepared by the Andean Mission with first-hand accounts

Peru: An Andean Country with Significant Disaster and Emergency Management Challenges, Heriberto Urby, Jr., J.D., Ph.D.1, David A. McEntire, Ph.D.2, Ekong J. Peters, 3

Peru earthquake of May 32, 1970; engineering geology observations, Lloyd S. Cluff, Bulletin of the Seismological Society of America

Earthquake-report.com May 31, 1970; the deadly Ancash/ Huascarán earthquake The Peruvian times, Yungay 1970-2009:

Remembering the tragedy of the Earthquake

Structural Behavior in the 1970 Peru Earthquake, Glen V. Berg and Raul Hunsid L.

www.ingramcontent.com/pod-product-compliance
Lightning Source LLC
Chambersburg PA
CBHW031317250726
48656CB00005B/1846